CRAFTS

FOR YOUR LEISURE YEARS

Cora Bodkin
Helene Leibowitz
Diana Wiener

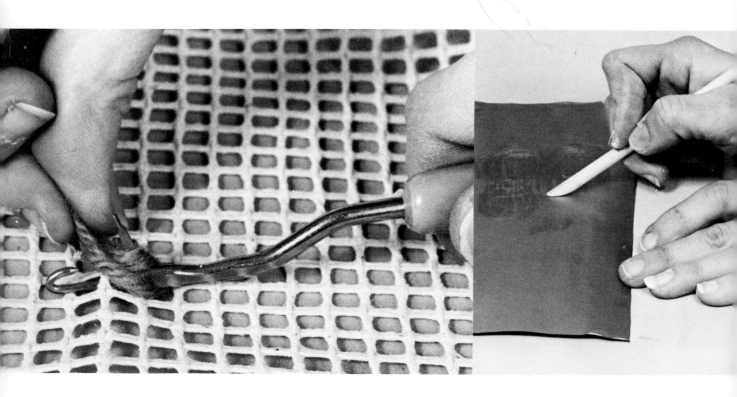

CRAFTS

FOR YOUR LEISURE YEARS

E 70 1

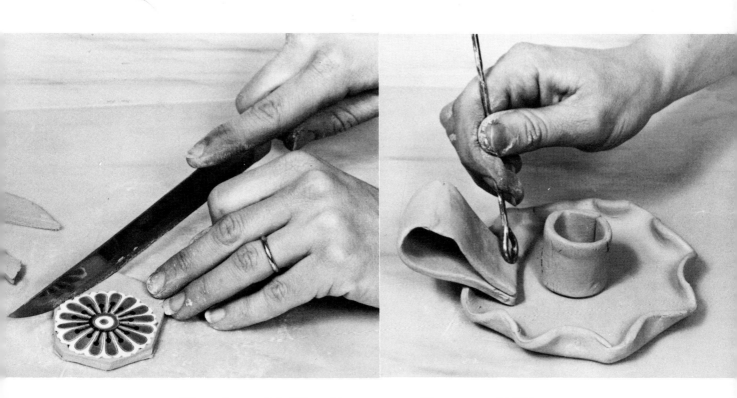

Houghton Mifflin Company   Boston   1976

Dedicated to the senior citizens
whose enthusiasm for crafts inspired us.

Book design by Sandie Starr Lahan, Starr Graphics

Library of Congress Cataloging in Publication Data

Bodkin, Cora.
Crafts for your leisure years.
Bibliography: p.
1. Handicraft. I. Leibowitz, Helene.
II. Wiener, Diana. III. Title.
TT157.B663   745.5′02′40565   76-29636
ISBN 0-395-24767-5   ISBN 0-395-24837-X pbk.

Printed in the United States of America

M 10 9 8 7 6 5 4 3 2 1

ACKNOWLEDGMENTS

We thank the following people who invited us to observe and discuss their arts and crafts programs at senior centers, nursing homes, and rehabilitation hospitals where they are employed as occupational therapists, physical therapists, recreation leaders, and arts and crafts instructors: Marsha Frankenstein, Carol Greenbaum, Carolyn Louridakis, Mr. Mann, Della Moser, Sol Satin, Mrs. Schook, Gerry Wasserman, and Mrs. Zachrone.

Special thanks also to our editor, Frances Tenenbaum, for assisting and encouraging us, to Lillian Modell for her patient and efficient typing of the manuscript, to photographer Charles C. Prusik for working around the clock (and teaching us some carpentry as well), and to Harold E. Yourke of Art and Frame of Rockland for teaching us the tricks of the graphic art trade.

Most of all, thanks to our husbands, Jerry, Marty, and Ira, for putting up with countless lonely nights and trying days of babysitting, supporting, and cooperating with us so that we could write this book.

CONTENTS

Chapter 5   page 161   MAIL-ORDER SUPPLIES

Chapter 1

CRAFTS FOR OLDER ADULTS

ALMOST FORTY MILLION AMERICANS — nearly 19 per cent of the population — are over the age of fifty-five. They have reached the time of life when they are either retired or are beginning to think about it. Even working people, with the responsibilities of raising a family behind them, have time to embark upon new interests and new activities.

Of all the leisure-time activities one can pursue in later life, none is more satisfying than a hobby that involves creating with your hands. Yet unlike the younger generation, which is growing up with crafts as a part of their lives, many older people have never tried their hand at creating with wood, or clay, or paints, or wool, or any other craft materials. And never having done so, they are often reluctant to try new skills for fear of frustration and failure.

But there is an added irony. Just when they *have* the time to become involved in craft activities, many people have some disability that (they assume) prevents them from working with their hands or eyes. More than three out of every four persons over sixty-five have one or more chronic conditions of aging, including arthritis, palsy, stroke, or visual impairment.

At sixty-eight Mrs. Leonard (not her real name) fits both of these categories. She is a widow who lives alone, and although her general health is excellent, her hands are badly swollen and partially crippled with arthritis. The skin on her fingertips is cracked and extremely sensitive.

At her senior citizen center she enjoyed the companionship — "It's so depressing to sit at home alone" — but although she liked to watch the arts and crafts group, she resisted all invitations to join. "So what was I going to do with a tiled ashtray, me a confirmed non-smoker? Why should I get my hands all messy and waste my time doing that kindergarten work?"

Even as she said it, though, Mrs. Leonard knew that she was afraid to try something she had never done before. Besides, even if she had been willing to "look foolish," her hands wouldn't let her try.

One day the crafts group was working on kitchen plaques, something Mrs. Leonard particularly loved. "I wanted to make one so badly that the teacher noticed it and urged me to try. I explained that this was something I really couldn't do because it meant cutting out felt and my fingers are too swollen to fit in a scissors. But the teacher insisted and showed me something called an X-acto knife. She wrapped some foam rubber around the handle and taped the foam into place. I was able to hold the tool comfortably and I managed to cut the felt with that knife. My daughter was so pleased with the plaque that she hung it up in her kitchen right away."

For Mrs. Leonard that plaque was just the beginning of a new world of activity, of gifts to make — "So what if I don't need an ashtray; I can always give it away" — projects to work on with her grandchild, presents to bring her friends. "I'm always thinking about what I am going to make next, and I'll tell you, it's a good thing to be able to do something you enjoy, to keep busy, and not always worry about your troubles. If I can do this work today, then this day is worth living."

Crafts for Your Leisure Years is directed primarily to the millions of older adults who either have never learned a craft or who would like to explore new ones. In addition, it is written for the thousands of professionals and volunteers — like us — who have found it difficult, if not impossible, to find appropriate, interesting projects for their crafts groups.

The projects in this book are geared to men and women of different tastes, interests, and levels of ability. They are the ones we have found to be most popular. And while they are definitely not designed as projects for the handicapped, people with handicaps *can* do them by using one or more of the compensatory techniques described and illustrated in chapter two. So if your hands are shaky, or your eyesight isn't too keen, or you have arthritis, or one hand is disabled, you will be able to perform all sorts of crafts techniques you may have thought impossible before.

Our crafts projects do not require expensive equipment or materials — in fact, whenever possible, we recommend recycled materials. You will find everything you need at home, or in variety, lumber, or hardware stores, or through the mail-order suppliers listed in chapter five. Occasionally the name and address of the supplier of a specific item is given within the text of a chapter. This is done whenever the specific item is not available through any of the general mail-order suppliers. The value of your finished products will far exceed the cost of the materials, which makes them especially nice for gifts or bazaar items.

All of the materials we have used have been screened for safety and do not have objectionable odors. In chapter three, "Basic Craft How-To's," we have included two comprehensive charts on adhesives and finishing materials. These charts will help you make sense of the bewildering variety of glues, cements, stains, and paints on the market by telling you exactly which to use on what. Under the lists of materials needed for each project, adhesives and finishing materials are preceded by an asterisk (*). Please refer to the charts for detailed information on handling these materials.

In this same chapter of basic craft how-to's, we have also described

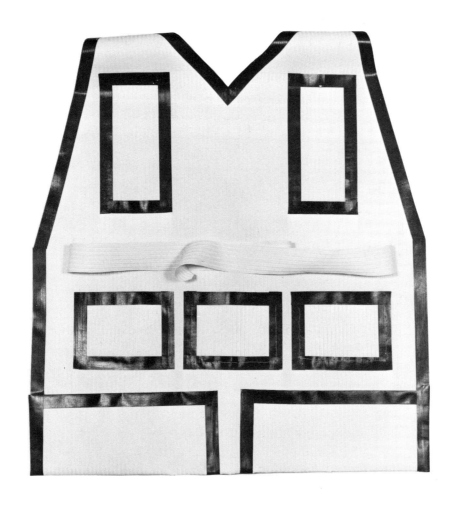

FIGURE 1

and illustrated every tool and technique needed to complete the projects in this book. Here you will learn exactly how to use hand tools, sand wood, paint, blend paint colors, trace and transfer patterns, and select and thread sewing needles.

If you've never been a "craftsperson," here are some general rules and suggestions that will help you get the fullest enjoyment from your new hobby.

Before you start any project, read through the project materials and instructions. Assemble all of the materials you will need.

Select a well-lit place to work and cover your worktable with newspaper. Prop this book in a convenient spot so that you can follow the steps as you work. (You may want to make the Tabletop Bookstand (page 126) as your first project!)

Wear a waterproof apron that has several pockets to hold tools or other supplies. We suggest you make one by recycling an old flannel-backed tablecloth. Cut a neck opening and armholes. Cut out pockets from extra material and attach them with self-stick tape. (Fig. 1)

Above all, allow yourself plenty of time. Relax and enjoy what you are doing. Crafts projects cannot be rushed. Designs look sloppy if they are done carelessly, and paints and glues require adequate time to dry. All of these projects can be done at several sittings, so stop working before you get tired or uncomfortable. You will be glad to return to your work later on. Anyway, it is much more rewarding to work slowly than to rush through a project and then be so displeased with the results that you have to do it over again — or, worse, give up.

We are sure that this book will be just the beginning of a new world of crafts for you, and that after you have mastered the techniques involved in our instructions, you will go on to work out new variations and your own ideas. We'd like very much to hear from you and to know how you are doing. Please write to us at:

P.O. Box 285
Spring Valley, New York 10977

Chapter 2

COMPENSATORY TECHNIQUES AND USEFUL TIPS

When the three of us began to work with our crafts groups in senior citizen centers, one of the first things we discovered was how difficult it was to locate appropriate projects; the ones we found in books and magazines were either too complex or too costly — or too childish. Looking for help, we visited colleagues in many other senior citizen centers and discovered that although many of them were arts and crafts teachers, they were at as much of a loss as we were. Furthermore, since none of them had any training in working with the elderly, they did not know of compensatory techniques that would enable people afflicted with the disabilities of age to overcome their handicaps. We then went to institutions that employed occupational therapists who had this training, and with their help we devised the compensatory techniques in this chapter. (Actually, in spite of their training, these professional workers had difficulty finding enough interesting and challenging projects for the elderly or disabled. We hope that the ones we have worked up for this book will help them solve their problems too.)

THE TECHNIQUES

If your hands are shaky or your eyesight weak, or you have arthritis or have lost the use of one hand, or your skin is sensitive, here are some techniques and tips that will enable you to perform all sorts of crafts techniques.

1. Use masking tape to fasten paper, fabric, cardboard, or other thin flat items to your worktable. (Fig. 1)
Aid for: one-handed
        palsied
        arthritic

2. Attach suction cups to the bottoms of plates, cups, jars, and bottles that you are decorating. They are also useful for bottoms of paint jars and the like to avoid knocking over and spilling.
Especially useful are suction soap holders. (Available in supermarkets and hardware stores.) (Fig. 2)
An equally suitable substitute is modeling clay (available in toy stores), floral putty (available in florists' shops) or Super Stuff.* (Fig. 2)
Aid for: one-handed
        arthritic
        palsied
        visually handicapped

FIGURE 1

FIGURE 2

FIGURE 3

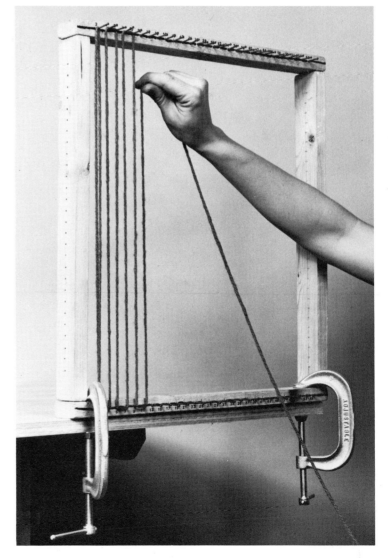

FIGURE 4

FIGURE 5

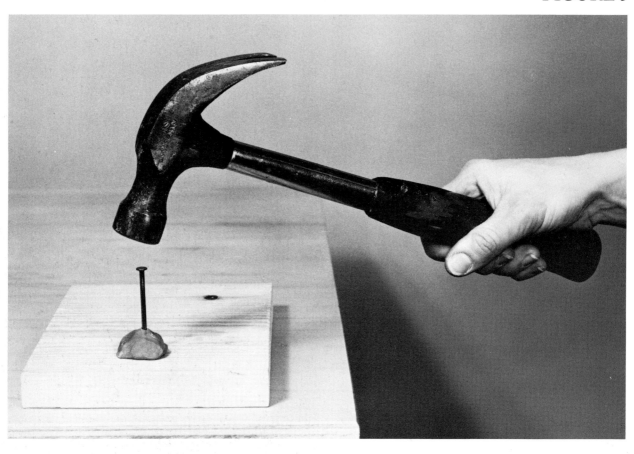

3. Use C clamps to fasten looms, stretcher frames, weaving frames, etc., to the worktable, holding the frame in a convenient, upright position. (Fig. 3)
Aid for: one-handed
        arthritic
        palsied
        visually handicapped

4. Hold work for sewing by attaching one edge of the work to a table with masking tape and weighting down the work in your lap with a book or other suitable object. (Fig. 4)
Aid for: one-handed
        arthritic
        palsied

5. Place a small lump of clay or putty on the spot in which a nail or tack is to be hammered. Set the nail or tack into the clay to hold the nail in place. Hammer in the nail. Remove the clay or putty. (Fig. 5)
Aid for: one-handed
        palsied
        arthritic

6. A craft vise-lacing pony is held by placing both legs over the base while seated on a chair. This vise holds your work steady. Especially suited for supporting needlepoint on plastic canvas. (Fig. 6) Available from Tandy Leather Company, 1001 Foch, Fort Worth, Texas 76107. (817-335-4161)
Aid for: one-handed
        palsied
        arthritic

FIGURE 6

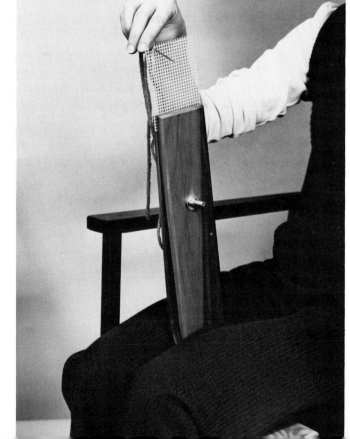

7. Build up the handles of tools and utensils such as paintbrushes, screwdrivers, utility knives, crochet hooks, etc., by wrapping sponge or foam rubber around the handle until it is a comfortable width. Tape the foam firmly into place. Tape the end of the foam to the tool handle to avoid slipping. (Fig. 7)
Aid for: arthritic
         skin-sensitive

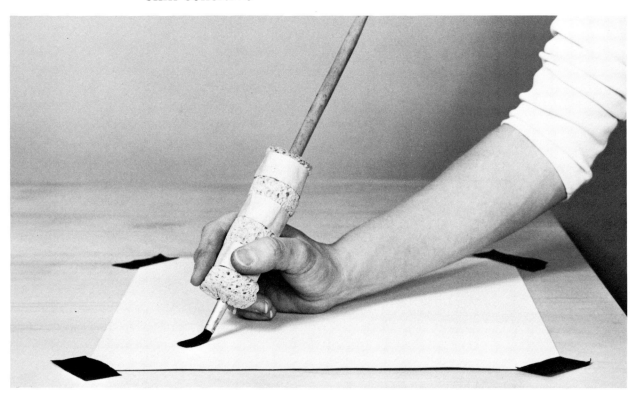

FIGURE 7

8. Build up the arm of a chair to a comfortable working height by taping foam or folded towels to the top of the chair arm. Hand-shaking is reduced to a minimum when the elbow is supported on the chair arm. (Fig. 8)
Aid for: palsied

9. To cut paper or fabric, insert the paper or stiff fabric into the center of a thick book and cut with bent-handled scissors. (Fig. 9)
Aid for: one-handed
         arthritic
         palsied

10. To avoid skin abrasion, attach sandpaper to smooth blocks of wood with tacks, or use sanding blocks available in hardware and paint stores. (Fig. 10)
Aid for: arthritic
         skin-sensitive

FIGURE 8

FIGURE 9

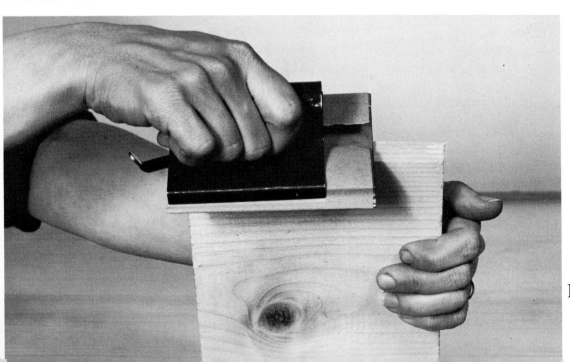

FIGURE 10   13

TIPS FOR PEOPLE WITH VISUAL HANDICAPS

1. Work in bright colors.

2. Use thick yarns and large-eyed needles.

3. Select simple patterns with large areas of color and little detail. Abstracts are particularly suitable.

4. Investigate the market of assorted aids such as magnifiers that clip onto eyeglasses, magnifiers on stands (some with lights attached), magnifiers worn around the neck. Consult your physician as to the suitability of any of these aids for you. These magnifiers are available from art supply distributors such as Arthur Brown and Brother, Inc., New York Central Supply Company, Irving Berlin, Inc., Cloder Corporation (see chapter five for addresses of suppliers).

5. Develop your sense of touch by experimenting with those crafts that are particularly suited to people with vision problems: working with clay, weaving, and mosaic tile work are examples.

6. When purchasing a craft product, ask the salesperson to read the label to you: warnings, instructions, and directions for opening and closing the container.

TIPS FOR PEOPLE WITH ARTHRITIS

1. Electric scissors are easier to use than hand scissors.

2. Macrame, rug hooking, weaving, and working with clay are particularly good exercises for the fingers.

3. Knitting and crocheting are poor activities for arthritics because the fingers are held stiffly for long periods of time.

4. Handles of tools can be built up to avoid the necessity of holding the fingers in a tight grasp. (Technique #7, p. 12.)

TIPS FOR PEOPLE WITH SENSITIVE SKIN

1. Use plastic gloves, preferably the thin disposable surgical type, for any messy work. (Available by mail order from Spencer Gifts, 1601 North Albany Avenue, Atlantic City, New Jersey 08411 — 609-345-3141).

2. Use acrylic yarns, not wool.

3. Avoid handling abrasives such as sandpaper.

4. Use a hand cream to keep the skin as supple as possible.

TIPS FOR PEOPLE WITH RESPIRATORY AILMENTS

1. Work in a well-ventilated room.

2. Use water-based paints and adhesives that have no objectionable odors or harmful fumes. The applicators (brushes, sponges, cloths) for these products are cleaned in water, thus eliminating the use of harmful thinners such as turpentine.

3. Avoid projects involving sanding unless you can work out-of-doors or in a room with an exhaust fan. Use a mask as added protection against inhaling dust.

4. Avoid all aerosol products.

Chapter 3

BASIC CRAFTS HOW-TO'S

ALL OF THE TOOLS and basic techniques necessary for completing the projects in this book are in this chapter. Before starting a project be sure to read the section relevant to it. In addition, much of the information here will also be useful for any craft and any craftsperson — in particular the charts on adhesives and finishes, which are a source of confusion even to experienced people. We think you will want to refer back to this chapter often.

CARPENTRY TOOLS AND INSTRUCTIONS

TOOLS NEEDED FOR PROJECTS

claw hammer
screwdriver
crosscut saw
coping saw
putty knife
awl
utility knife
hand drill
sandpaper
countersink
C clamps

HOW TO USE THE HAND TOOLS

CLAW HAMMER

This hammer comes in two sizes — the 16-ounce is for general work and the 13-ounce is for light work.

To hammer a nail, hold the nail between your thumb and forefinger at a right angle to the board. Hold the hammer with your other hand near the end of the handle for the greatest driving power. (Fig. 1) One tap is needed to start the nail into the board. Continue hammering with medium strokes until the head of the nail nears the board. Finish hammering with light strokes. For the one-handed, palsied, or arthritic, see compensatory technique #5 (page 11) to help you stabilize the nail.

To pull out a nail, use the claw end of the hammer and pull on the head of the nail until the nail is about ¾ inch out. At this point, a ½-inch block of wood can be inserted under the hammer and against the nail for leverage and to prevent marring the board as you continue to pull the nail. (Fig. 2)

FIGURE 1

FIGURE 2

19

SCREWDRIVER

The screwdriver we use has a flat head for screws with a single slot. To put in a screw, hold the screwdriver handle firmly in the palm of your hand and grip the neck of the handle firmly with your thumb and forefinger. (Fig. 3) The tip of the screwdriver should be as wide as the screwhead and should completely fill the screw slot. NOTE: The application of liquid soap to the threads of the screw makes the screw easier to insert.)

CROSSCUT SAW

The crosscut saw is used to make cuts across the grain. Place the board to be cut on your worktable and hold it securely with your left hand (right hand if left-handed). Allow about a 3-inch clearance between the cut and the worktable so that you won't cut into the table. Hold the crosscut saw at about a 45-degree angle to the board. (Fig. 4)

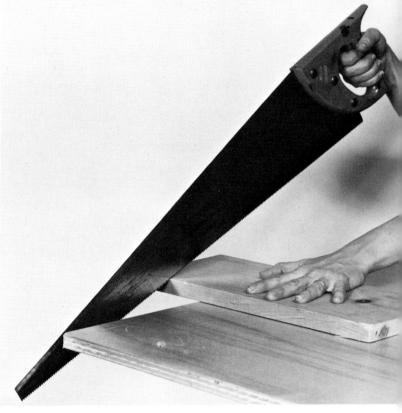

FIGURE 4

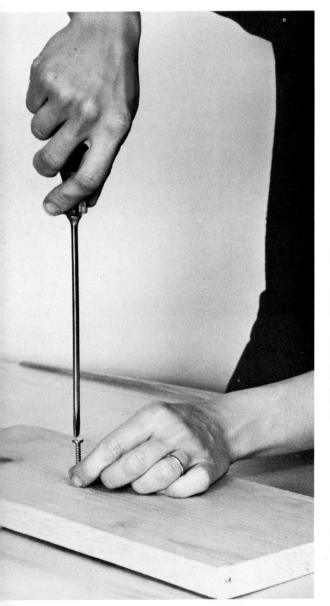

FIGURE 3

COPING SAW

The coping saw is a curve cutter. (Fig. 5) It has a narrow flexible blade that can be changed when it becomes dull.

PUTTY KNIFE

The putty knife is a flat knife with a straight tip used for spreading grout, cement, pastes, etc. (Fig. 6)

AWL

The awl has a sharp pointed head for making and starting holes in wood and other materials. (Fig. 7)

FIGURE 5

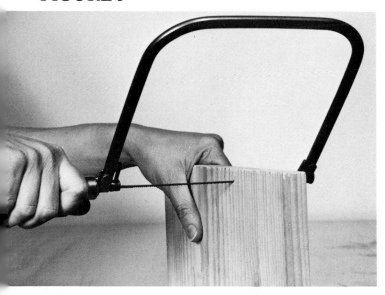

FIGURE 7

FIGURE 6

21

UTILITY KNIFE

The utility knife has a razor blade for a tip that can be changed when the blade becomes dull. The utility knife is good for cutting through corrugated cardboard, mat board, etc. Use a metal yardstick as a straightedge to guide the knife. (Fig. 8) Select a utility knife with a broad handle that provides a firm grip and a blade that can be retracted into the handle when not in use.

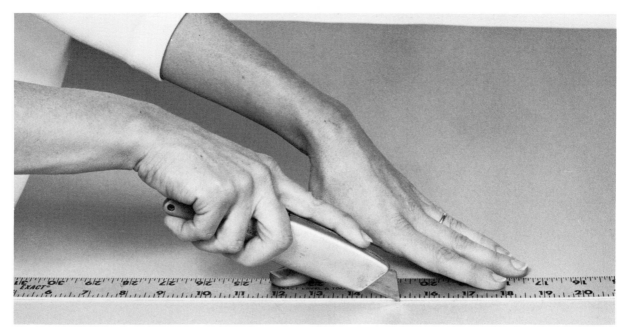

FIGURE 8

HAND DRILL

To drill a hole, start the hole with an awl (punch or ice pick) so that the drill won't slip. Keep your pressure even and turn the handle of the drill slowly. (Fig. 9) A tip to remember when drilling holes is that when you drill through a board, stop as soon as the bit breaks through on the other side. Then turn the board over and complete the hole from that side. This step prevents the wood from splintering.

SANDPAPER

Sand with the grain of the wood for a smooth finish. Do not sand across the grain or in a swirling motion or you will tear the fibers of the wood. (Fig. 10) Start with medium sandpaper unless the board is very rough, in which case start with coarse sandpaper. The sanding block is a holder for the sandpaper. The block improves the contact between the abrasive and the wood being sanded and also prevents your hand from being scraped.

FIGURE 9

FIGURE 10

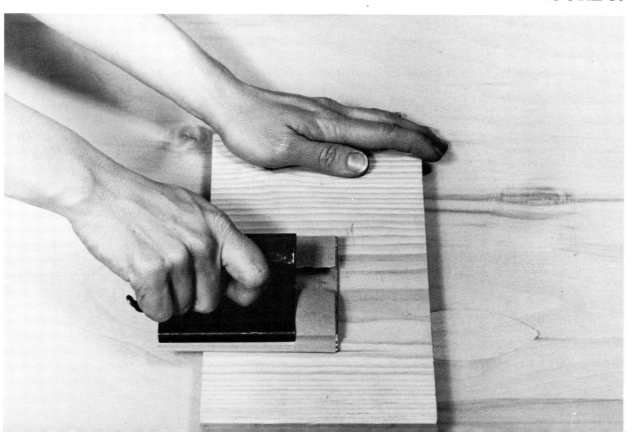

23

COUNTERSINK

After a nail or brad has been hammered into a wood surface, a countersink can then be used to sink the nail below the surface. The hole can be filled with wood glue or wood putty to hide the nail. (Fig. 11)

C CLAMPS

A C clamp is a metal device shaped like the letter C with a screw threaded vertically through the bottom that can be adjusted to accommodate objects of various sizes. The C clamp attaches objects to a stable work surface, allowing such objects to be sawed, nailed, screwed, drilled, etc. (Fig. 12) C clamps come in various sizes. For the projects in this book, we recommend 3-inch C clamps. More than one clamp can be used at a time. To hold an object vertically at the edge of the worktable, use a second clamp to support the first clamp to the worktable. (Fig. 13)

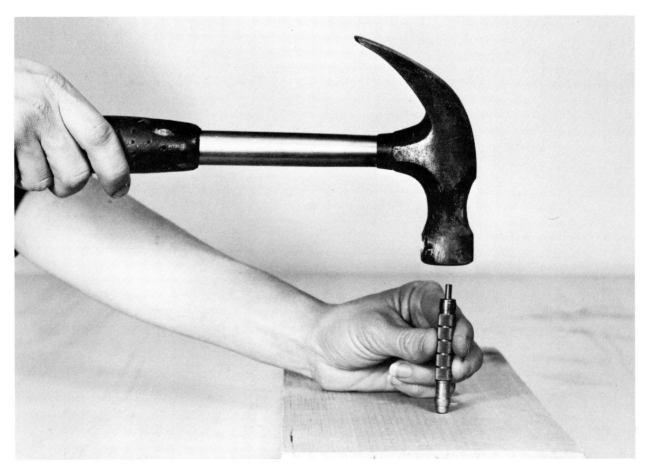

24   FIGURE 11

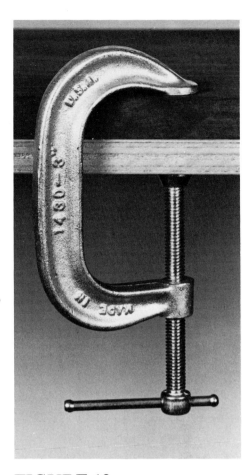

FIGURE 12

FIGURE 13

HOW TO PAINT

Use a stirrer to mix paint to a smooth consistency and uniform color. Stretch a rubber band crosswise across the top of the paint container. You will wipe the side of the bristles of the brush against the rubber band so that the excess paint will drip back into the paint container. To avoid having paint drip down onto your work surface, we recommend that you tape a paper plate to the bottom of the paint container. Dip the bristles of the brush only halfway into the paint. If necessary remove excess paint as described above. When painting, use long steady strokes.

25

HOW TO BLEND PAINT COLORS
(Use the color wheel, Fig. 14, on opposite page as a guide)

The three primary colors are red, blue, and yellow. They are so called because they cannot be produced by any mixture of pigments. See the color wheel to note the placement of red, yellow, and blue.

The secondary colors are mixtures of two of the primaries. Red + blue = purple; red + yellow = orange; blue + yellow = green. Note the placement of orange, green, and purple on the color wheel. SEE THE COLOR WHEEL FOR MIXING AN ENDLESS VARIETY OF COLORS.

To mix a tint or lighten any color, start with white. Then add your color until the desired tint is achieved.

To mix a shade or darken any color, add black drop by drop. The paint darkens quickly so work carefully.

You will note that there are arrows on the color wheel. These arrows point from one color to its direct opposite. For example, the opposite color from red is green. These opposites are known as complementary colors. In order to dull any color, add its complement drop by drop until you have achieved the desired color.

HOW TO TRACE AND TRANSFER PATTERNS

TRACING PAPER

Translucent white tracing paper is easy to see through, durable, tear resistant, and it withstands erasures. Tracing paper is purchased on 50-sheet pads measuring 9 by 12 inches or 14 by 17 inches, or rolls 18 by 24 inches, and is available at stationery stores, art supply stores, and general arts and crafts suppliers.

HOW TO USE TRACING PAPER

1. Lay the tracing paper over the pattern to be copied. The tracing paper must be held firmly in place so that it won't shift. Use four paper clips (one at each corner) to attach the tracing paper to the design to be copied.

2. Use a sharpened pencil or ball-point pen to go over the outline of the design on the tracing paper. Avoid pressing down hard on your pen or pencil to prevent making impressions on the original design that is being copied.

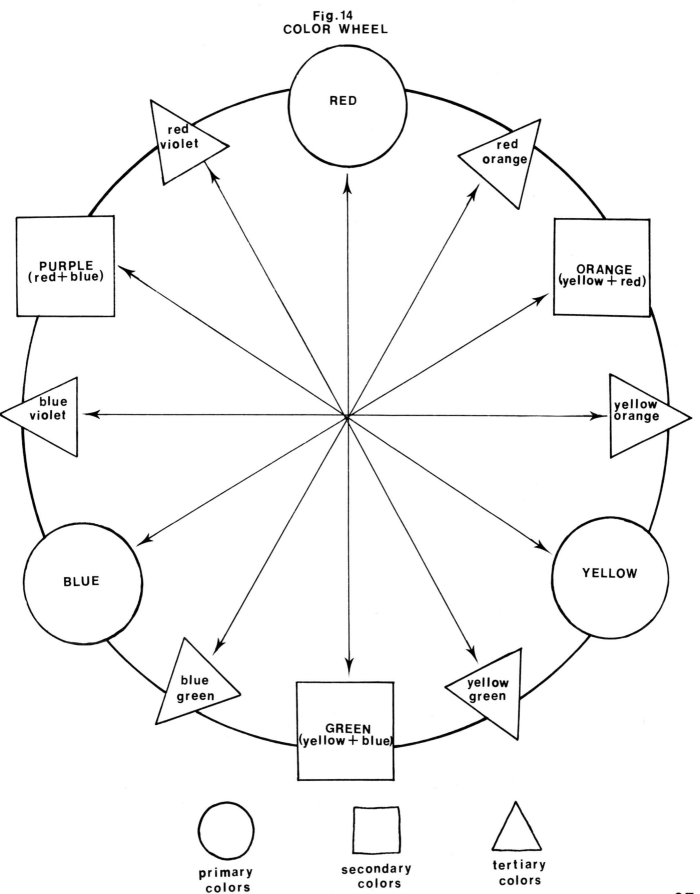

Fig.14
COLOR WHEEL

RED

red violet

red orange

PURPLE
(red+blue)

ORANGE
(yellow+red)

blue violet

yellow orange

BLUE

YELLOW

blue green

GREEN
(yellow+blue)

yellow green

primary colors

secondary colors

tertiary colors

27

3. Remove two of the paper clips and carefully lift the tracing paper from the design being copied. Compare the tracing paper copy with the original design for completeness and accuracy. Make any necessary additions or corrections.

HOW TO TRANSFER THE TRACED DESIGN

1. Cut out your traced pattern outline.

2. Pin or tape the traced pattern onto the desired surface or material.

3. With the appropriate pen, pencil, or marker, outline the design onto the desired surface or material.

4. Cut out the outlined design.

HOW TO SELECT AND THREAD SEWING NEEDLES

KINDS OF NEEDLES

CHENILLE NEEDLES have sharp points and range in size from numbers 13 to 26, with #13 the largest needle. Numbers 13, 14, and 15 are good for rug yarn; numbers 16, 17, and 18 are good for knitting worsted; numbers 19 and 20 are good for crewel. Chenille needles are usually used for sewing on fabric.

TAPESTRY NEEDLES have blunt points. The size range is the same as for chenille needles. Tapestry needles are usually used for working on needlepoint or rug canvas.

HOW TO THREAD YARN THROUGH A LARGE-EYED NEEDLE

MANUAL LOOP TECHNIQUE

1. Hold the lower half of the needle between the thumb and forefinger of your right hand. Loop the yarn around the needle, leaving a 3-inch end. (Fig. 15)

2. Pinch the yarn loop between the thumb and forefinger of your left hand. At the same time, pull against the yarn loop with the needle to give it tautness. (Fig. 16)

NEEDLE THREADING
MANUAL LOOP TECHNIQUE

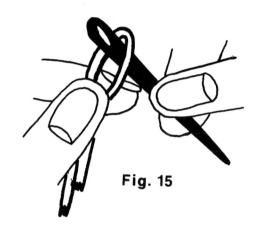

Fig. 15

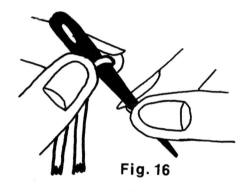

Fig. 16

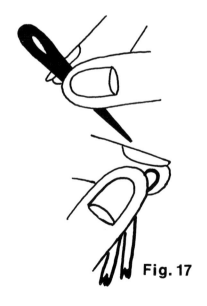

Fig. 17

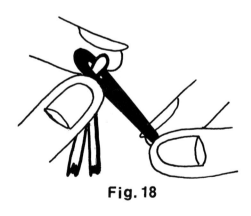

Fig. 18

3. Lift the needle with your right hand. Keep the yarn loop pinched in your left hand. (Fig. 17)

4. With your right hand, push the eye of the needle over the yarn loop. Pull loop completely through. (Fig. 18)

**NEEDLE THREADING
MANUAL PAPER TECHNIQUE**

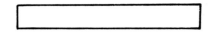

Fig. 19

Fig. 20

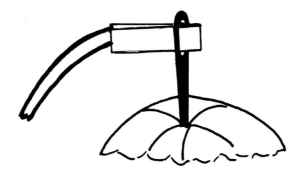

Fig. 21

MANUAL PAPER TECHNIQUE

1. Cut a paper strip 2 inches long and ¼ inch wide. (Fig. 19)

2. Fold the strip in half, inserting the end of the yarn between the two layers. (Fig. 20)

3. Thread the folded paper strip through the needle's eye. (Needle may be stabilized if you wish.) (Fig. 21)

MECHANICAL NEEDLE-THREADER FOR YARN

"Thread-It," manufactured by Ozburn-Janesville Corporation, Janesville, Wisconsin 53545. (608-754-0317) This needle-threader is the only mechanical threading aid for yarns we have come across that is easy to use. (Fig. 22, right)

AUTOMATIC NEEDLE-THREADER FOR SEWING THREAD

The only needle-threader we have seen, designed to thread small-eyed needles with sewing thread, that a person with visual handicaps can handle is the Hexe Automatic Needle-Threader. This needle-threader is available by mail order from the American Foundation for the Blind, 15 West 16th Street, New York, New York 10011. (212-924-0420) (Fig. 22, left)

FIGURE 22, LEFT   FIGURE 22, RIGHT

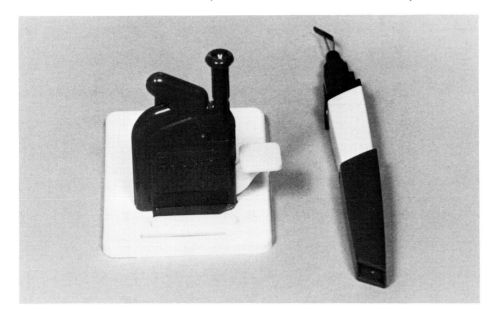

31

ADHESIVES

This chart includes products that we have recommended and used in our projects. These products are odorless, nonirritating, easy to apply, nonflammable, and require a simple soap and water clean-up.

TYPE OF PRODUCT TRADE NAME	GENERAL PURPOSE	HOW TO USE
White general-purpose adhesive: Sobo Elmer's Glue-All (Many others, marketed under various trade names)	Good glue for paper, fabric, leather, cork, and wood when applied to a rigid surface	Twist open applicator top, squeeze gently, and apply to surface that is to be glued. (Don't glue onto porous surfaces such as fabric and felt. Smooth glue with finger or brush on nonporous surfaces.)
Paste-form white cement: Tacky Bond–484 Extra Tacky	Good for adhering fabrics, felt, leather, metal, glass, styrofoam and some plastic	Apply with finger or craft stick
Decoupage glue: Poly Coupage Royal Coat Decoupage Finish Art Podge Mod Podge	Seals, glues, glazes decoupage work. Milky white when wet, dries transparent	Brush on with paintbrush
China/glass cement: Elmer's Glue-All	Waterbase cement repairs ceramics, glass, tile, even fine china	Squeeze thin line from tube along surface to be glued
Alithatic resin glue: Hobby Model Wood Glue	Unexcelled for wood. Tough and sandable. Will not gum up sandpaper	Squeeze bottle. Spread heavily on both surfaces. Clamp or weight. Can be applied and spread with applicator tip
Multipurpose, heavy-duty adhesive: Touch N Glue	For bonding metals, ceramics, plaster, wood, brick, canvas, concrete, leather, glass, fabric to themselves or each other	Apply adhesive to one clean, dry surface. Press to second surface immediately. Separate parts when possible for five minutes to speed up initial holding strength. Press together firmly. Wait several hours before applying weight to bonded parts

ADVANTAGES	AND DISADVANTAGES	SOURCES (Where no address is given, see Chapter 5, Mail-Order Supplies)
Odorless Quick-setting Dries clear Soap and water clean-up	Not flexible when dry Not waterproof	Supermarkets Hardware stores All craft supply stores
Odorless Suitable for bonding to flexible or rigid surfaces Soap and water clean-up Stronger bond than liquid white glue	Not waterproof Rim of jar and inside of lid must be cleaned thoroughly to prevent lid sticking to jar	Hardware stores Bond Adhesive Company 120 Johnston Avenue Jersey City, New Jersey 07303 201-333-1460 Triarco
Odorless Soap and water clean-up	Finish not waterproof	Hardware stores S & S Arts & Crafts American Handicrafts Dick Blick Company Boin Arts & Crafts Bergen Arts & Crafts J & A Handy-Crafts
Odorless Dries clear and quickly Soap and water clean-up		Hardware stores Dick Blick Company
Sandable (will not gum up sandpaper) Odorless Soap and water clean-up Very strong bond Dries to natural wood color	May not be used on photos, bare metals, or surfaces affected by water or excessive heat	Hardware stores Bond Adhesive Company 120 Johnston Avenue Jersey City, New Jersey 07303 201-333-1460
Nonflammable Nontoxic Nonsniffable Water-resistant Soap and water clean-up	Heavy parts need overnight support	Hardware stores Champion International Corporation Chemware Group Weldwood Packaged 2305 Superior Street Kalamazoo, Michigan 49003 616-381-1100

ADHESIVES (continued)

TYPE OF PRODUCT TRADE NAME	GENERAL PURPOSE	HOW TO USE
Reusable adhesive gum: Super Stuff	To use as a stabilizer to prevent objects from sliding	Tear off generous blob. Warm it by kneading, pulling, and stretching. Roll it into a ball. Place between the two surfaces to be fastened and press hard. To remove: pull it away gently or roll it off
Wall mount strips: Franklin Self-stik wall mount strips	Mount pictures and accessories where nails, hooks, and other hangers are not practical. Can mount on wood, brick, or tile	Peel necessary number of strips from their white backing and press firmly to back of picture frame or accessory. Keep strips near the outside edges that make contact between frame and wall. Remove transparent backing from other side of all strips. Press firmly against wall in exact location desired
Carpet tape: Twin Stik double face tape Super-stik double face tape Anchor double face tape Mystik double face tape	Adheres carpet tiles, mats, linoleum. Mounts posters and photographs to paper, glass, metal, rubber, plastic wood	Peel one side of lining paper and place it on surface of article to be glued. Peel off other side of lining paper and place article on surface to which article will be glued
Double-sided masking tape: 3M Tuck	Suitable for mounting anything lightweight	
Double-stick cellophane tape: Scotch brand	Suitable for mounting anything very lightweight	Pull desired length of tape from dispenser. Apply on surface of article to be glued
Concentrated bonding adhesive: Weldbond	For bonding all porous and nonporous materials except some types of plastics and rubber	Plastic squeeze bottle. Concentrate is diluted according to specific directions depending upon objects to be bonded. The longer the adhesive is allowed to dry, the stronger the bond

ADVANTAGES	AND DISADVANTAGES	**SOURCES** (Where no address is given, see Chapter 5, Mail-Order Supplies)
Reusable Nontoxic Odorless Nonstaining	Surfaces must be clean and dry	Hardware stores USM Corporation Consumer Products Division P.O. Box 1139 Reading, Pennsylvania 19603 212-921-2791
One strip will support half a pound of weight Easy to apply	Once installed, it cannot be removed without replacing strips Make sure all strips make firm contact with wall and accessory	Hardware stores Franklin Metal & Rubber Company 58 Jacksonville Road Hatboro, Pennsylvania 19040 215-542-7300
Very easy to apply No mess No drying time		Hardware stores Metalco Metal Tile Corporation 258 Herrick Road Mineola, New York 11501 516-741-7960
Same as carpet tape		Same as carpet tape
Same as carpet tape Packaged with a dispenser No lining paper to peel off		Stationery stores Hardware stores
Odorless Easy to use Soap and water clean-up Water-resistant Dries clear Quick-setting Nonflammable Strongest nontoxic glue we have tested	Cannot be used to bond objects exposed to hot liquids	Hardware stores Frank T. Ross & Sons, Incorporated Lawrence Avenue Toronto, Canada 416-282-1108

FINISHING PRODUCTS

NAME OF FINISH	CHARACTERISTICS	SURFACES APPLIED ON
Poster Colors or Tempera Colors	Colors arc opaque and dry flat. Can be mixed 1:1 with water and still retain color. Also available in powdered form which is easily mixed with water	Paper, wood, clay, poster and mat board, plaster and other porous surfaces
Latex Paint (flat or semi-gloss); interior or exterior	Colors are opaque. Dries rapidly, stain and mar-resistant, washable, thinned with water Flat paint dries with a mat finish. Semi-gloss dries with a shiny finish	Wood, walls, masonry, metal, plastic, plaster, clay, mat board
Acrylic Artist Colors — tube or jar	Colors are opaque. Tube colors have a low sheen, while jar colors dry mat. Thins with water and when dry is exceedingly durable, permanently flexible, and completely nonyellowing	Artists canvas, mat board, wood, plaster, clay, china
Acrylic Stain	Comes in wood tones that allow the grain of the wood to show through	Wood, clay, plaster
Polymer Gloss Medium	Can be used as a sealer and gloss varnish. Can also be used as a glue for decoupage	Clay, wood, plaster, mat board

HOW TO USE	ADVANTAGES AND DISADVANTAGES	SOURCES
Apply with a brush or sponge	Soap and water clean-up Easy to apply, inexpensive Powdered form can be kept indefinitely Only a mat finish Not a permanent finish unless covered with a sealer Tends to run	Stationery Stores Art Stores General Arts and Crafts Suppliers
Apply liberally with a brush. Spread evenly and quickly. Avoid rebrushing. Apply when temperature of air and surface are above 50° F	Soap and water clean-up Easy to apply. Can be thinned with water to the point that will give the effect of a stain, allowing wood graining to show Does need adequate ventilation	Paint Stores Variety Stores Hardware Stores
Apply tube colors with a brush or palette knife depending upon design. Apply jar colors with brush and use for all water-color techniques	Soap and water clean-up Easy to apply. Tube colors have the body and brushing quality of oil colors and will retain crisp textures Expensive	Artist Supply Companies Art Stores Larger Variety Stores General Arts and Crafts Suppliers
Apply with a lint-free cloth or a brush and then wipe off excess with a soft cloth. When working on wood, always apply and remove stain in the same direction as the grain of the wood	No objectionable odor Soap and water clean-up Nonflammable	Variety Stores Paint Stores General Arts and Crafts Suppliers
To use as a varnish apply liberally with a brush over painted or unpainted surface	Dries clear. Dries quickly No objectionable odor Soap and water clean-up Can remove a finish, so do a test piece first Not waterproof	Art Supply Stores General Arts and Crafts Suppliers

Chapter 4

THE PROJECTS

THE PROJECTS DESCRIBED IN THIS CHAPTER encourage creativity through a variety of activities for both men and women. The diversity of the projects appeals to many tastes and levels of ability.

The craft supplies needed to complete these projects are found in the home, at variety, lumber, and hardware stores, or through specified mail-order distributors listed in chapter five. The adhesives and finishes listed in the project materials are preceded by an asterisk (*) to indicate that additional information is available on the charts in chapter three.

EASY-TO-DO PROJECTS

The first project is the easiest, with each subsequent project requiring a little more skill and dexterity than the preceding one. Many projects in this group are suitable for children with adult supervision. Try some of these projects with your grandchildren when they are restless and bored.

LEATHER-LOOK VASE
(photo, page 157)

MATERIALS

glass jar
¾-inch masking tape
paste shoe polish (brown preferred)
cloth to apply polish
*polymer gloss medium and paintbrush
            (optional)

40

FIGURE 1

INSTRUCTIONS

1. Remove any labels and clean the jar thoroughly.

2. Turn the jar upside down; cover the bottom first with small pieces of masking tape, tearing them off and overlapping them as you go. (Fig. 1) Work your way up until the jar is completely covered with masking tape.

3. Rub paste shoe polish onto the jar with a cloth. (Brown shoe polish gives a leatherlike appearance.)

4. At this point the jar can be left as is, with a mat finish, or painted with a polymer gloss medium for a shiny finish. The jar is now ready for your favorite flowers.

41

VICTORIAN PICTURE GROUPING
(photo, page 157)

This frame provides a display of six 5 by 7-inch photos or prints — a great way to show off your favorite hobby or collection and perfect for your family photos. These frames are made from plastic picket fencing, which may be linked together to make larger displays.

MATERIALS

one 36-inch section of plastic picket fencing (manufacturer: Fordick Corporation, 2030 Grand Avenue, Kansas City, Missouri 64108 — 816-421-3314 — available in garden supply centers and hardware stores)
*latex paint
½-inch paintbrush
white bond paper
scissors
*paste-form white cement (preferred)
cardboard or mat board 8 by 30 inches, or two 8 by 15 inches
utility knife to cut mat board to size
pencil
newspaper
wax paper
*adhesive drops or wall mount strips
tracing paper
metal yardstick

INSTRUCTIONS

1. Cover work area with newspaper. Place wax paper over the newspaper to prevent sticking.

2. Lay the plastic frame wrong side up on wax paper.

3. With pencil trace the pattern for the large triangle on bond paper and cut out. Using this pattern, trace and cut 24 triangles. (See tracing instructions, page 26.)

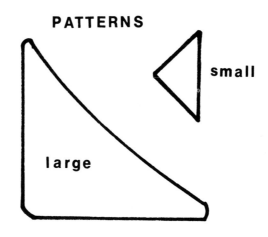

PATTERNS

small

large

4. Trace the pattern for the small triangle on bond paper and cut out. Using this pattern, trace and cut 12 triangles.

5. Using white glue, attach the triangles to the back of the frame to cover the open triangular spaces. Let glue dry completely.

6. Turn the frame right side up. Paint the entire frame in desired color, including the paper triangles. Let the paint dry completely. Give the frame a second coat of paint if necessary.

7. Measure and cut the cardboard or mat board to size — 8 by 30 inches (two 8 by 15-inch pieces may be substituted) — using a utility knife and metal yardstick.

8. Mount the pictures to be displayed on the mat board with paste-form white cement. (Fig. 1) As you work, overlay the frame to insure correct centering.

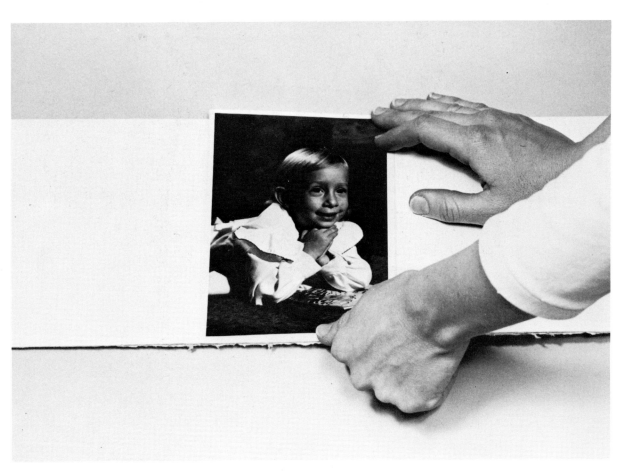

FIGURE 1

9. Tape or glue the mat board to frame.

10. Apply adhesive drops or wall mount strips to the back of the mat board.

Your Victorian Picture Grouping is now ready to mount on the wall.

MEXICAN MIRROR PLATE
(photo, page 157)

MATERIALS

approximately 2 ounces of rug yarn in 3 or 4 colors
(acrylic, nylon, or polyester; available by mail order
from Lee Wards or Wyco Products, or local yarn stores)
round heavy-pulp paper plate or oval heavy-pulp platter
*paste-form white cement
3 to 4-inch round mirror, or 4-inch square mirror, or 3 by
5-inch oval mirror (available through American Handicrafts Company)
scissors
toothpick
newspaper

INSTRUCTIONS

1. Cover work area with newspaper.

2. About 2 inches from top and sides make two holes 1 inch apart in the paper plate with the point of the scissors. (Fig. 1a)

3. Cut a 6-inch length of rug yarn. Thread the yarn through the holes so that the ends are in front and the loop is in the back of the plate. Do not tie ends. (Fig.1b)

FIGURE 1a

FIGURE 1b

FIGURE 2a

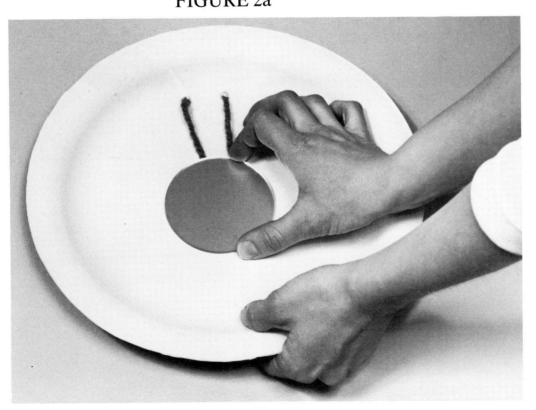

4. Cover the entire back of the mirror with a thin layer of paste-form white cement. Place the mirror in the center of the plate. Make sure the ends of the yarn are covered by the mirror and held securely. (Fig. 2a)

47

FIGURE 2b

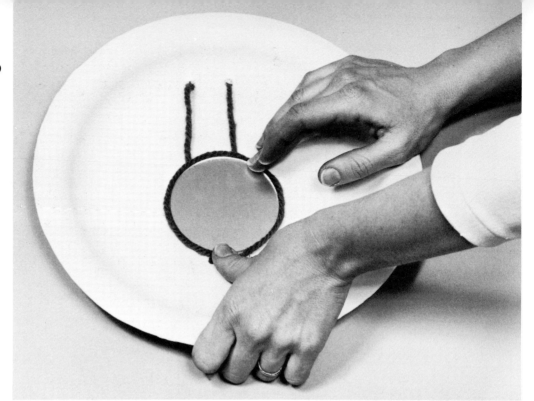

5. Apply a line of glue around the edge of the mirror. Take a strip of yarn and carefully surround the mirror so that all edges are covered. When the mirror is surrounded, cut the yarn with the ends overlapping slightly. (Fig. 2b)

6. The yarn lends itself to many interesting designs, so don't limit yourself to just going around and around. See diagrams of the sample design motifs. Proceed by applying the glue onto the plate section by section as you are ready to glue down the yarn. The entire plate should be covered with yarn when you are finished.

7. Yarn may be overlayed onto previous yarn layer to make a design.
NOTE: Use a toothpick to help position the yarn where desired.

DESIGN MOTIFS

square

coil

loop

48

STRAW WEAVING BELT

Photograph by Henry Tofte, Lumenphore, Ltd.

MATERIALS

one 70-yard skein of rug yarn
4 plastic straws with large openings
8 beads (large hole to accommodate rug yarn)
scissors
sewing needle with large eye
tape measure
knitting needle or skewer

INSTRUCTIONS

1. Using a tape measure, measure your waist. Add 20 inches.
After winding yarn into a ball, cut four strands of yarn to
this length.

49

2. Thread a strand of yarn through each straw, using a knitting needle to help push the yarn through. (Fig. 1)

3. Thread a bead onto the yarn at the top of the straw to prevent the yarn from slipping through. (Use a large-eyed needle if necessary.) Knot the yarn at top of bead. (Fig. 2) Repeat this step with the other three straws.

4. Place all of the straws in front of you on a table. With the end of the ball of yarn, tie a knot halfway around the right-most straw.

5. You are now ready to begin weaving. Holding the straws with beads in your left hand (or right hand if you are left-handed), take yarn in your right hand and put it behind second straw, in front of third straw, behind fourth straw. (Fig. 3)

6. Row 2: Bring yarn around front of fourth straw, behind third straw, in front of second straw, behind first straw. Row 3: Bring yarn around front of first, behind second, in front of third, behind fourth. Repeat these last two rows for belt. (Fig. 4)

7. When you have worked your way to the top of the straws, push your work downward off the straws onto the strands. This affords new working space. Keep working in this way, checking the length until you have reached the size of your waist. Knot and cut end.

8. When the belt is the proper length, take the end of the yarn at the top of the straw and pull it upward so that the yarn at both ends of the belt is even. These ends are used to tie the belt closed. With scissors, slit the straws and remove them.

9. Thread beads at bottom of each strand of yarn and knot. Both ends of the belt are now finished off with beads.

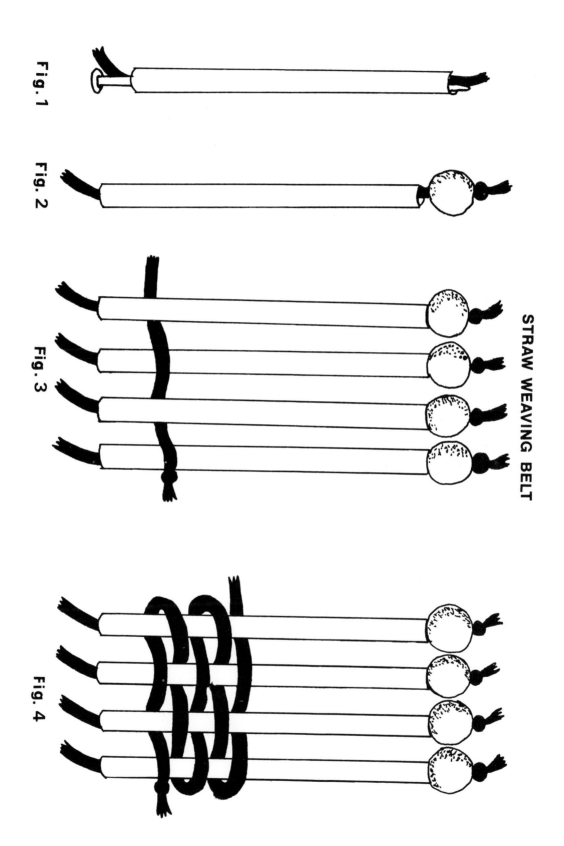

Fig. 1

Fig. 2

Fig. 3

Fig. 4

STRAW WEAVING BELT

51

PERSONALIZED PLATE PLAQUE
(Grandma's-Girl Plate) (photo, page 157)

MATERIALS

salad-size china plate (old or new) that has no center
   pattern
pink or flesh-colored felt for face and ears
yellow, black, or brown felt for hair
6-inch hair ribbon
black and red marking pens, fine point
*black acrylic paint
paintbrush #1
movable eyes, buttons, or sequins for eyes
scissors
tracing paper
pencil

INSTRUCTIONS

(Follow the same procedure for other plate designs.)

1. With a pencil and tracing paper trace and cut out pattern pieces for felt face and hair. (See tracing instructions, page 26.) Transfer and cut out designs on the felt.

2. Apply the glue to the reverse side of the felt face; spread with your fingers. Cover the entire surface.

3. Center the face on the plate and press down.

4. Place the felt hair around the face and glue down.

5. Glue eyes in place. With black marker draw two dots for the nose and with red marker make a small circle under nose for the mouth.

6. Make a bow with the ribbon and glue it to the hair.

7. With a small paintbrush and black acrylic paint, write GRANDMA'S across the top and GIRL across the bottom.

8. Hang the plate with a spring plate holder.

53

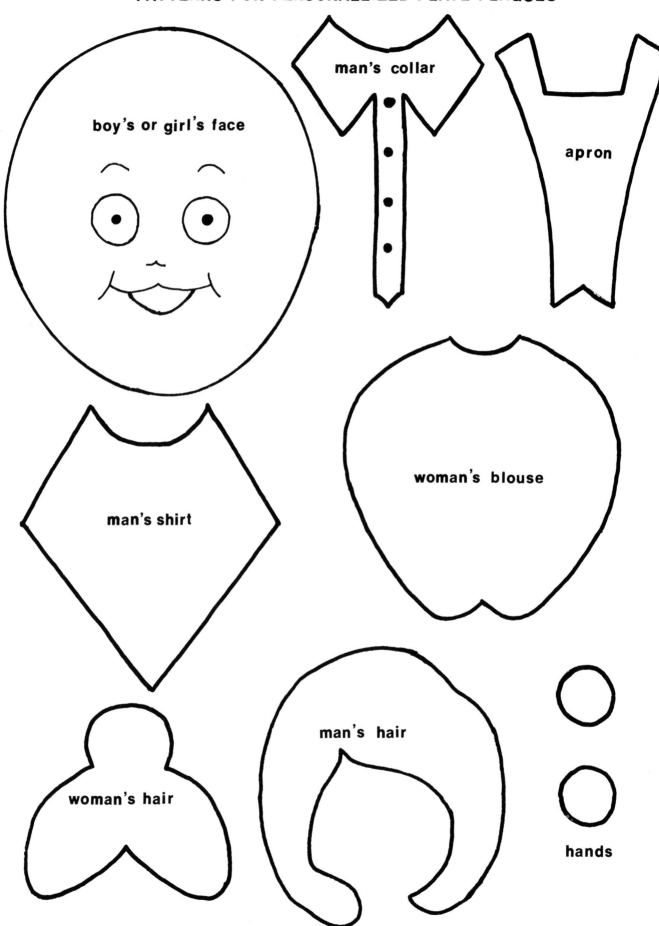

boy's or girl's face

man's collar

apron

man's shirt

woman's blouse

woman's hair

man's hair

hands

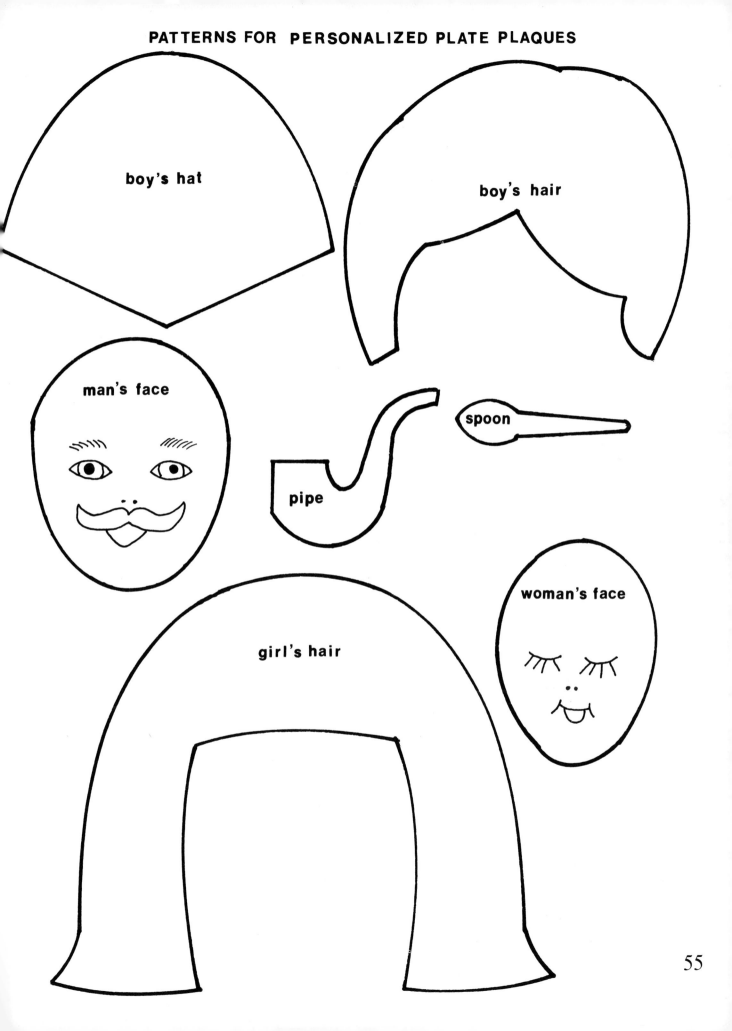

boy's hat

boy's hair

man's face

spoon

pipe

woman's face

girl's hair

HAT PINCUSHION
(photo, page 157)

MATERIALS

tracing paper
½ yard of lightweight opaque fabric (cotton or a cotton
    blend)
1½ yards of small size rickrack coordinated to fabric color
3-inch-diameter Styrofoam ball (available in variety stores
    and from general arts and crafts suppliers)
straight pins
cardboard
*white glue
small paintbrush
scissors
serrated knife
tape measure or yardstick
small cup for glue
newspaper

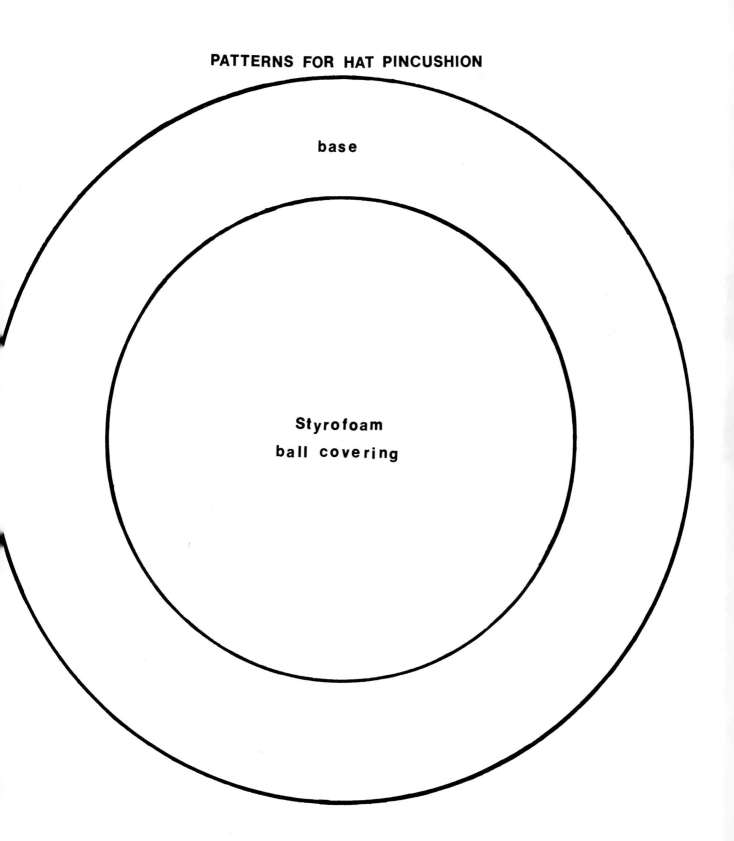

PATTERNS FOR HAT PINCUSHION

base

Styrofoam
ball covering

INSTRUCTIONS

1. Trace and cut out the patterns for the base of the pincushion and for the Styrofoam ball covering. You will have one large and one small solid circle patterns. (See tracing instructions, page 26.)

2. Lay the pincushion base pattern on the cardboard and trace around the outside with a pencil. Repeat this step. You should have two solid cardboard circles. With scissors, cut out both cardboard circles.

3. Spread newspaper over the work area.

4. Brush a thin layer of glue completely over one side of each cardboard circle. Put the two glued sides together, forming a double cardboard circle. Let the glue dry about five minutes.

5. Using the double cardboard circle as a pattern, trace and cut out two fabric circles.

6. Brush glue onto the wrong side of each fabric circle. Glue one fabric circle to one side of the cardboard circle and glue the other fabric circle to the other side of the cardboard circle. Let dry five minutes.

7. Trim off any excess fabric that may extend beyond the cardboard circle. Make all edges even.

8. Brush glue around the exposed cardboard edge of the fabric-covered base. Glue the rickrack around this edge until the entire edge is covered. Cut off the excess rickrack.

9. Lay the pattern for the Styrofoam ball covering on the fabric. Trace around the pattern and cut out one circle with scissors.

10. With a serrated knife, ''saw'' the Styrofoam ball in half.

11. Cover one of these halves with the fabric circle. (The other half is not needed.) Pull the fabric as taut and as smooth as you can around and underneath the half ball, using the

straight pins to secure the fabric. These pins do not have to be removed from the Styrofoam. This fabric-covered piece of Styrofoam will be the top of the pincushion.

12. Brush glue onto the flat bottom of the top of the pincushion.

13. Center the top of the pincushion on the base of the pincushion. Let dry thoroughly.

14. Brush glue along the edge where the pincushion base and top meet.

15. Glue the rickrack around this edge and cut away the excess. Let dry thoroughly.

16. With scissors, cut a 24-inch piece of rickrack and make a bow in the center, leaving two long ends.

17. Brush glue onto the knot of the bow and attach the bow to the pincushion at any point where the pincushion base and top meet. Secure the bow with a straight pin. Do not remove this pin. Let dry five minutes.

The pincushion can now be worn around your neck for your convenience. Because this pincushion has a flat bottom, it can be placed on a table and used as a stabilizer for holding a needle when threading it.

KITCHEN WALL ORGANIZER/BULLETIN BOARD
(photo, page 157)

MATERIALS

tracing paper
pencil
ball-point pen
   (black preferred)
scissors
straight pins
yardstick
two sheets of corrugated cardboard glued together (18 by
   24 inches), or one piece of Homasote (18 by 24 inches),
   available at lumber dealers and building suppliers
*concentrated bonding adhesive (Weldbond)
small paintbrush
small dish to hold the adhesive
calendar pad
*double-sided carpet tape
felt: 18 by 24 inches for background — color A
      two 9 by 12-inch squares for canister lids — color B
      one 9 by 12-inch square for canister lids, salt and
         pepper shaker lids, and rolling pin handles —
         color C
      12 by 26 inches for border and shelves — color D
      one 9 by 12-inch square for salt and pepper shakers and
         rolling pin — color E

60

INSTRUCTIONS

1. Trace all pattern pieces onto tracing paper with a pencil and cut out. (See tracing instructions, page 26.)

2. Cut background color-A felt to 18 by 24 inches.

3. Attach double-sided carpet tape to all four sides of cardboard or Homasote. Place two additional strips of carpet tape horizontally 9 inches from top and 6 inches from bottom for additional support of canister pockets. (Fig. 1)

4. Position felt background onto the cardboard or Homasote. Pull the felt taut and press firmly over carpet tape to insure good adhesion.

PATTERNS FOR KITCHEN WALL ORGANIZER/BULLETIN BOARD

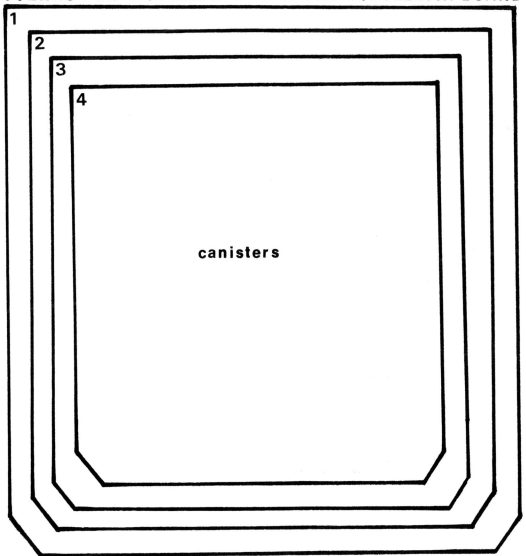

canisters

5. Pin four canister patterns, two onto each color-B felt square. Outline the patterns in ball-point pen onto felt. Cut out patterns.

6. Pin four canister lid patterns, two shaker top patterns, and two rolling pin handle patterns onto color-C felt square. Outline the patterns in pen, and cut out.

7. Pin scallop pattern on color-D felt. Outline pattern in pen. Continue moving pattern piece along until border measures 20 inches long. Repeat. Make two additional borders measuring 26 inches long in the same manner.

8. Cut two pieces of color-D felt ¾ by 18 inches for shelves.

9. Pin shaker pattern on color-E felt. Outline pattern in pen. Cut out. Repeat. Pin rolling pin pattern on color-E felt. Cut out. Cut a centered horizontal slit to insert calendar.

10. In ball-point pen, print:
    "Letters" on the largest canister
    "Bills" on second largest canister
    "Coupons" on second smallest canister
    "Pad" on smallest canister

11. Measure and mark 9 inches down from the top of the bulletin board at both ends. With the yardstick and ball-point pen draw a horizontal line connecting these markings.

12. Measure and mark 6 inches from the bottom of the bulletin board at both ends. With ball-point pen draw a horizontal line connecting these markings.

13. Squeeze concentrated bonding adhesive into a small container. Brush full-strength adhesive onto one side of the felt shelf pieces. Turn the shelf pieces over and position them onto the background felt on the lines previously drawn.

14. Pin all other pattern pieces in their proper positions onto background felt as indicated in the photo.

15. Glue on all pieces in color-C felt.

PATTERNS FOR CANISTER LIDS

4 canister lid

3 canister lid

2 canister lid

1 canister lid

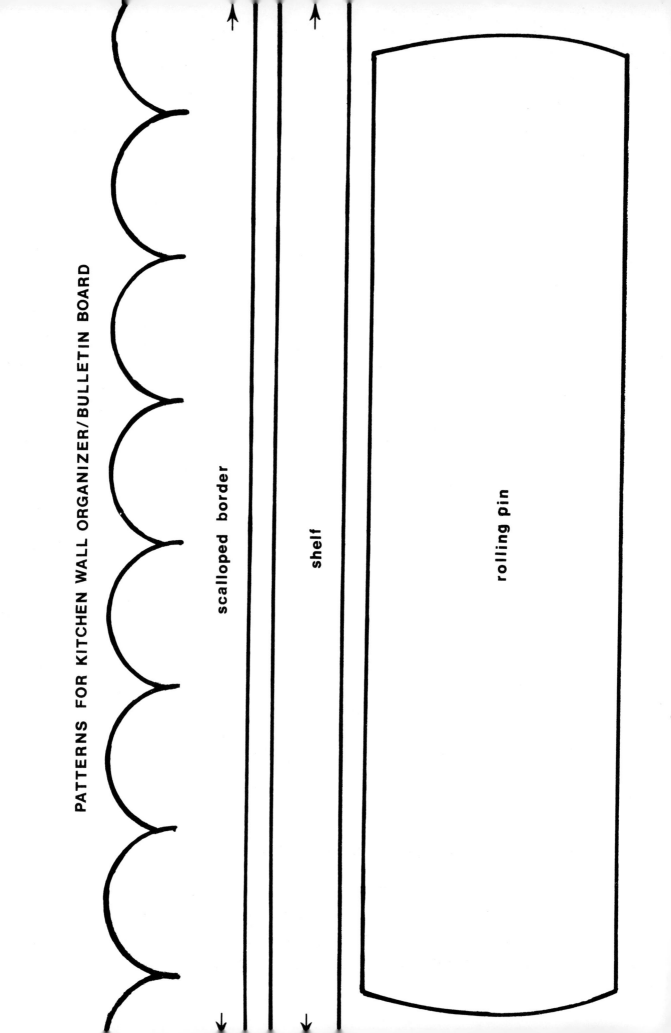

PATTERNS FOR KITCHEN WALL ORGANIZER/BULLETIN BOARD

scalloped border

shelf

rolling pin

64

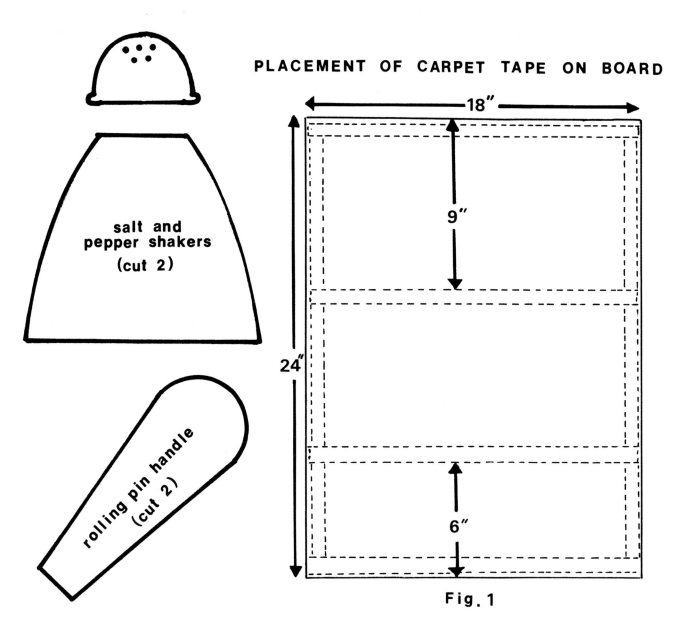

PLACEMENT OF CARPET TAPE ON BOARD

salt and pepper shakers (cut 2)

rolling pin handle (cut 2)

18"

9"

24"

6"

Fig. 1

16. Apply adhesive to bottom and sides only on four canisters and two shakers. Glue into place.

17. Apply adhesive to all four sides of rolling pin. Glue into place.

18. Glue on four pieces of scalloped border.

19. Slip calendar into slot on rolling pin.

2(. Double-sided carpet tape may be used to mount cardboard-backed Kitchen Wall Organizer to the wall. Screw eyes and wire may be used to mount the Homasote-backed Kitchen Wall Organizer to the wall.

TILE CANDLESTICK
(photo, page 157)

MATERIALS

tall, narrow bottle (such as an olive bottle)
tiny mosaic tiles (⅜-inch square) available at
    general arts and crafts suppliers
grout
container for mixing grout
spoon for mixing grout
newspaper
sponge
*paste-form white cement

water

unlined paper
scissors
ruler
toothpick
paper towel
small putty knife or rubber spatula
plastic gloves

INSTRUCTIONS

1. Coat the bottle with a thin layer of paste-form white cement. Apply it with your fingers as it is too thick for a brush. Wear plastic gloves if your skin is sensitive.

2. Make a paper pattern sheet for the bottle as follows:
    a. Cut a sheet of unlined paper to the height of the bottle below the neck.
    b. Wrap the paper around the bottle below the neck. Fold back the excess paper where the sheet overlaps. (Fig. 1)
    c. Cut off the excess paper.

FIGURE 1

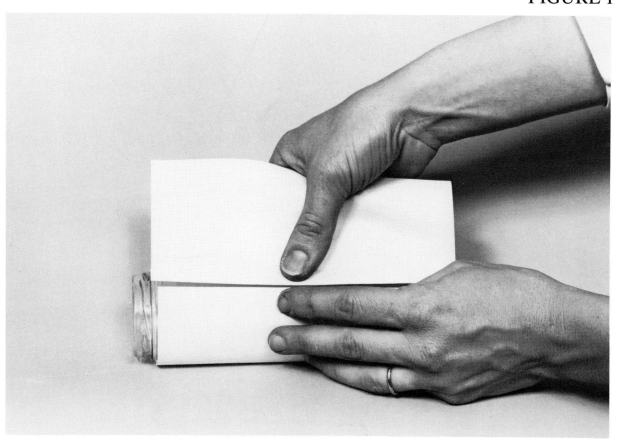

3. Lay the paper flat on a table and plan your mosaic design on this paper. Lay the tiles in the desired pattern, allowing small spaces between the tiles to accommodate the grout. Remember, the paper is the same size as the bottle you will be covering, so do not leave a border, but work the pattern so that it covers all of the paper.

4. Now you are ready to apply the tiles to the bottle. Cover the worktable with newspaper. Apply paste-form white cement to the bottom 1½ inches of the bottle. Position the bottom row of tiles, spacing them evenly. Remember to leave a small space the width of a toothpick between the tiles to accommodate the grout. Position the second row of tiles. Apply glue to another 1½ inches of the bottle and position tiles for the next two rows as described above. Continue these steps until you have finished covering the bottle to its neck. Check over the entire bottle and reposition any tiles that may have shifted out of place. Allow the glue to dry thoroughly (about six hours). Check all the tiles and if necessary reglue any loose ones.

5. Now you are ready to apply the grout. We suggest that you wear plastic or rubber gloves to avoid direct handling of the grout. Note that grout is alkaline on contact with water and can be irritating to eyes and skin. However, with proper handling it is safe to use.

Mix ½ cup of powdered grout by adding small quantities of water at a time and stirring constantly until you have achieved the smooth consistency of softened cream cheese. (If your mixture gets too loose, add small quantities of powdered grout.) Rinse the grout off the spoon with water. Scoop up the grout with the putty knife and rub into the cracks between the tiles. Make sure you fill in all the cracks completely. Do not worry about covering the tiles as you will wash them off later. Cover the entire neck of the bottle with grout. Apply more than one coat of grout if necessary. While the grout is still moist and pliable and you are wearing plastic gloves, take a damp sponge and wipe away excess grout, revealing all the tiles. (Fig. 2) Rinse the grout from the sponge as you work. Inspect your tiled bottle and add more grout if necessary. Clean the rim of the jar with the sponge and allow the grout to dry thoroughly overnight. Polish the tiles with a dry paper towel.

6. Your candlestick is ready for a candle. If the neck of the jar is too wide for a standard candle, wrap modeling clay arnd the base of the candle. A candle that is too wide may be trimmed to fit the neck of the tiled bottle.

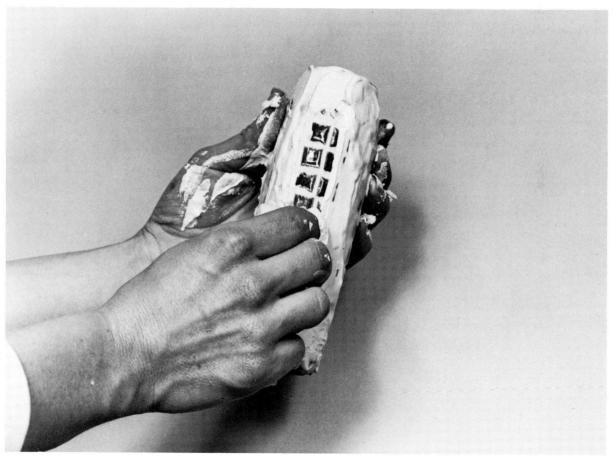

FIGURE 2

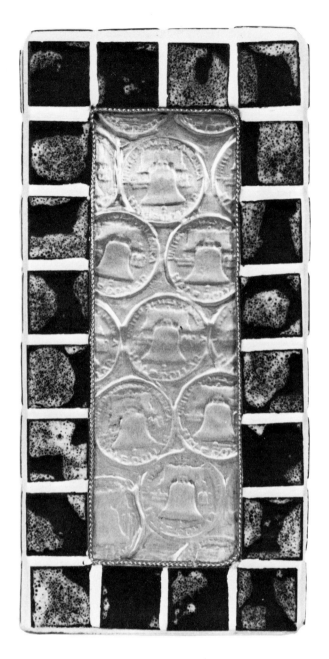

TOOLED FOIL AND TILE BOOKENDS
(photo, page 157)

MATERIALS (for two bookends)

two bricks
mosaic tiles to cover 2 square feet (each tile no wider
    than 1 inch)
two pieces of tooling foil 2 by 6 inches, any color, 36 or
    38 gauge (available at general arts and crafts suppliers)
one 10 by 12-inch felt square
4 feet of gold braid

wooden modeling stick
masking tape
stiff-bristled brush, any size
toothpick
*paste-form white cement (regular white glue may be
     heated in a pot over a low flame until it forms a paste
     consistency)
scissors
small putty knife
grout
container for mixing grout
paper towels
wax paper
water
plastic gloves
assorted coins (dimes, nickels, quarters)

INSTRUCTIONS (make both bookends simultaneously)

1. Cover the worktable with wax paper. Dust off the bricks
with a stiff-bristled brush.

2. Mix thoroughly 1 cup of powdered grout with
approximately ½ cup of cold water added a little bit at a time
until the grout is the consistency of softened cream cheese.

3. Wearing plastic gloves, seal the brick by applying the
grout with a putty knife to all sides of the brick except the
bottom — one of the smallest sides of the rectangle. Apply
the grout in a thin, even coat and allow to dry thoroughly.

4. Using masking tape, tape the coins closely together onto
the back of the sheet of tooling foil.

5. Turn the foil sheet right side up. Using a modeling stick,
rub firmly over the coins until a clear impression of the coin
design appears on the tooling foil. (Fig. 1)

6. Without bending the foil sheet, remove the tape and coins
from the back of the tooling foil.

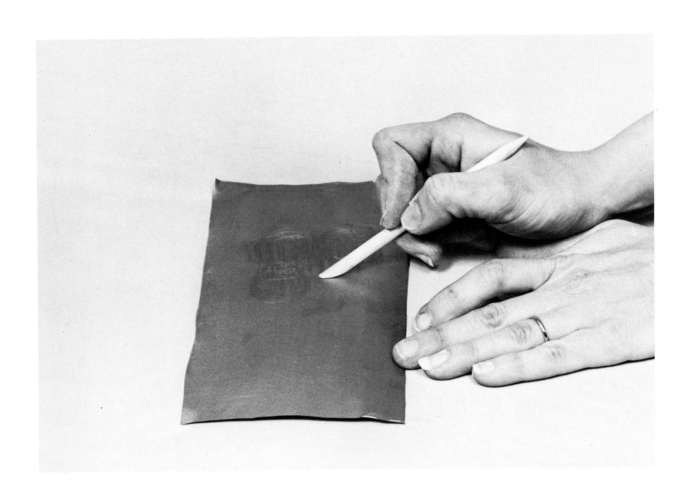

FIGURE 1

7. Apply a thick coat of paste-form white cement to the back of the tooled foil sheet and center the sheet on the front side of the bricks. Press the foil sheet firmly into place.

8. Lay the bricks on their backs. Position the mosaic tiles around the foil panel in the desired pattern. Remember to allow ample space between the tiles to accommodate the grout (the space should be the width of a toothpick).

9. Remove the tiles one at a time. Apply paste-form white cement to the backs of the tiles and reposition them one at a time. Allow the adhesive to dry thoroughly.

10. Lay the brick on one side. Position and glue the mosaic tiles in the desired pattern as described in steps #8 and 9.

11. Repeat step #10 on the other side of the brick.

12. Repeat step #10 on the top of the brick.

13. Thoroughly mix 1½ cups of powdered grout with approximately ¾ cup of cold water, adding the water to the grout a little at a time until the grout becomes creamy smooth.

14. Protect your hands with plastic gloves, and apply the grout to the tiled bricks with a putty knife, filling all the spaces between the tiles with grout.

15. While the grout is still moist and pliable, remove any excess from the surface of the tiles and foil sheet with a damp sponge. Rinse out the sponge with water as you work.

16. Allow the grout to dry thoroughly.

17. Polish the mosaic tiles with paper towels.

18. To adhere gold braid around the foil panel, apply paste-form white cement to the edge of the tiles and grout along the edges of the foil panel.

19. Press gold braid along the glued edges of the tiles, making a decorative border around the foil panel. Trim the end of the gold braid with scissors.

20. Place the bottom of the brick on the felt and trace the outline. Place the back of the brick on the felt and trace the outline.

21. Cut out the pieces of felt and glue them onto the back and bottom of the brick with paste-form white cement.

NOTE: These bookends may be used as doorstops, too.

PROJECT SUGGESTION: Coordinate a decorative planter to the bookends by covering a box constructed of 1-inch lumber with a tooled foil panel and mosaic tile.

CLAY PROJECTS

All of the clay projects described in this book are made out of a nontoxic self-hardening clay that is air dried, thereby eliminating the need for a kiln. The clay that we used is Marblex by Amaco — American Art Clay Company Inc., 4717 West 16th Street, Indianapolis, Indiana 46222. (317-244-6871) This clay (or similar self-hardening clays) is available in five-pound boxes from general arts and crafts suppliers.

Marblex is a gray self-hardening clay in moist form. Water may be added to make the clay more pliable. While this clay makes permanent objects without firing, these objects are not waterproof. We recommend that the objects be cleaned by dusting or vacuuming.

In our experience with this clay, we found that the clay object must be of a relatively uniform thickness to dry properly. Dry your finished pieces at room temperature (not in direct sunlight) and turn the pieces a couple of times a day.

We have included several projects using self-hardening clay because we wanted to give you a variety of ideas to make worthwhile use of the five pounds of clay. One box of clay will be enough to make all of these projects and many more.

CERAMIC TOOTHPICK OR MATCH HOLDER
(photo, page 158)

MATERIALS

ball of self-hardening clay about the size of an apple
*poster paint
*polymer gloss medium
paintbrush
rolling pin
wax paper
sharp-pointed knife
scissors
small container of water
leather thong or nails for hanger
two 12-inch rulers or ¼-inch-thick furring strips
barbecue skewer or knitting needle
tracing paper
pencil

INSTRUCTIONS

1. With pencil and tracing paper, trace paper pattern for back of Match Holder and cut it out. (See tracing instructions, page 26.)

**PATTERNS FOR
CERAMIC TOOTHPICK OR MATCH HOLDER**

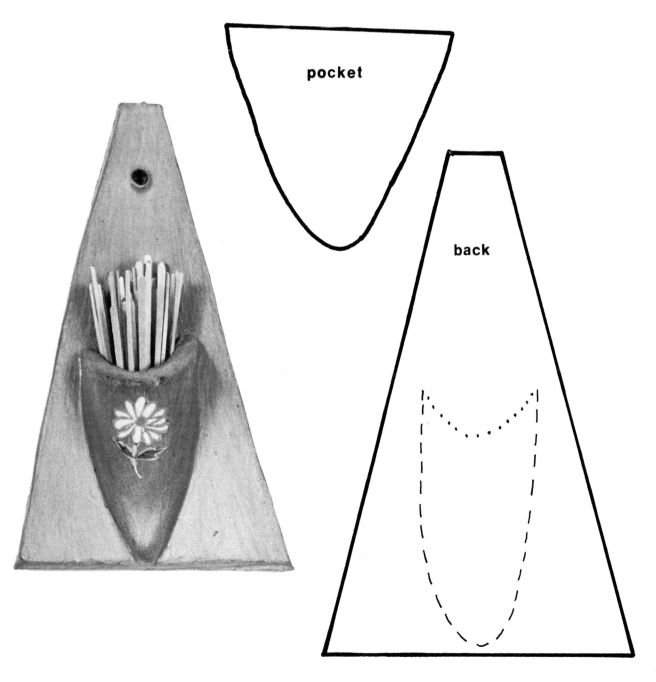

pocket

back

2. Trace the paper pattern for the pocket and cut it out.

3. Roll the clay into a ball between your two flattened palms.

4. Place clay on wax paper and flatten the ball with the heel of your hand.

5. Roll out the clay with the rolling pin supported at both ends by rulers or furring strips ¼ inch thick. (Fig. 1) The rolled-out clay should be larger than the pattern.

6. Place the paper pattern on the rolled-out clay. Cut away the excess clay with a knife. Save the trimmings for later use. (Fig. 2)

7. Smooth out the edges with moistened fingers.

8. Form a smaller ball and roll it out as above.

9. Place the paper pattern on the rolled-out clay. Cut away the excess clay with a knife.

10. Join the pocket to the base by making the edge of the pocket very wet; to attach the inside of the pocket use more clay and press it in with a skewer. (Fig. 3) Smooth the seam again with fingers until it feels like one piece of clay.

11. (Optional) Insert piece of crumpled wax paper in pocket to keep it open.

12. Dip your finger into the water and smooth out the area where you pressed the pocket into the base, making sure there are no cracks. Dip your fingers into the water again and smooth out the whole base around the edges. Again make sure there are no cracks. If cracks are left in the base, the piece may crumble when it dries.

13. Decide how the piece will hang on the wall and with the pointed end of the paintbrush make one hole.

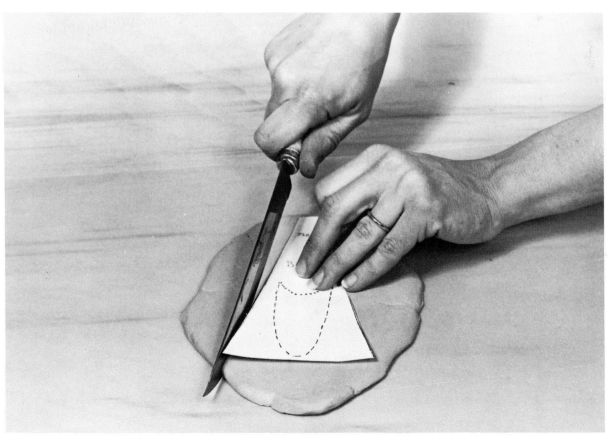

FIGURE 2

14. Keep the project on wax paper and allow it to dry indoors at room temperature for three days.

15. Decorate with paint. Allow the paint to dry thoroughly for one hour and then coat the piece with polymer gloss medium. (This step produces a ceramic effect.)
NOTE: *Polymer gloss medium brushes on milky white but dries crystal clear.*

Your Match Holder is now ready to be hung.

OTHER FINISHES

1. Food coloring may be used instead of paints. The colors are not as vivid as paints, but they do a good job.

2. Liquid shoe polish is another possibility. Brown produces earthy tones, red gives a mat finish. Blue is very dull.

Whatever finish you decide to use, the completed piece should be coated with polymer gloss medium to give it a ceramic effect.

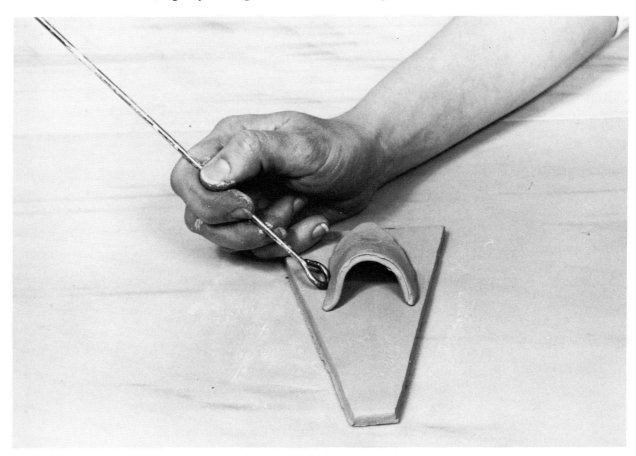

SINGLE-POCKET WEEDY
(photo, page 158)

MATERIALS

self-hardening clay (ball about the size of a large apple)
rolling pin
two 12-inch rulers or ¼-inch-thick furring strips (available
    at lumber dealers)
wax paper
knife
water in small container
paintbrush
*tempera paint (red and yellow)
container for blending paint
brown liquid shoe polish
*polymer gloss medium

INSTRUCTIONS

1. Roll the clay into a ball between your two flattened palms.

2. Place the clay on wax paper and flatten the ball with the heel of your hand.

3. Roll out the clay with the rolling pin supported at both ends of rulers or furring strips ¼ inch thick. (See Match Holder, Fig. 1, p. 76.)

4. Using the knife, cut the clay into a freeform shape. (Save the trimmings for later use.)

5. Smooth out the edges with moistened fingers.

6. Form a smaller ball and roll out as above.

7. Using a knife, cut the clay into a pocket shape.

8. Smooth out the edges with moistened fingers.

9. Join the pocket to the base by making the edge of the pocket very wet; to adhere the inside of the pocket use more clay and press it in with a skewer or nail. Smooth the seam again with fingers until it feels like one piece of clay.

10. Insert a crumpled piece of wax paper into the pocket to keep it open.

11. Dip your finger into water and smooth out the area where you pressed the pocket into the base, making sure there are no cracks. Dip fingers into the water again and smooth out the whole base around the edges. Again make sure there are no cracks. If cracks are left in the base, the piece may crumble when it dries.

12. Decide how the piece will hang on the wall and with the pointed end of the paintbrush make a hole(s).

13. Keep the project on wax paper and let it dry at room temperature for three days.

14. Blend red and yellow tempera paint to make a bright orange color, or use any other color of your choice.

15. Paint the back of the ceramic piece. Allow to dry (approximately a half-hour).

16. Paint the front and sides of the ceramic piece and allow to dry.

17. To give your piece an antique finish, cover it completely with brown liquid shoe polish. Wipe off the excess. Allow to dry.

18. Seal the finish with a coat of polymer gloss medium, front and back.

Your Weedy is ready to receive a dried flower/weed arrangement.

FREEFORM TRIPLE-POCKET WEEDY
(photo, page 158)

MATERIALS

self-hardening clay
skewer or nail
brown liquid shoe polish
wax paper
water
*polymer gloss medium
knife
small paintbrush

INSTRUCTIONS

1. Form a ball of clay the size of a large apple.

2. On the wax paper, flatten the ball with the palm of your hand.

3. Press the clay with your fingers until it is the desired thickness — ¼ to ½ inch — and size.

4. With the knife, cut the clay to a freeform design.

5. Make a hole with the skewer or nail in the desired spot to use for future hanging.

6. Make pockets by pressing fingers into small wads of clay. Vary the size and shape of the pockets. Add the pockets as described in directions for Match Holder, page 77, instruction #10.

7. After the ceramic piece has dried thoroughly — 72 hours — color the back with brown liquid shoe polish and allow to dry.

8. Color inside and out the front, sides, and pockets with brown liquid shoe polish. Allow to dry.

9. Scrape off polish with a knife along border, edge, and tops of pockets, revealing natural clay.

10. Paint the back of the ceramic piece with polymer gloss medium. Allow to dry.

You're ready to decorate your Pocket Weedy with dried weeds and flowers.

FLUTED COLONIAL CANDLESTICKS — Wrought-Iron Finish (photo, page 158)

MATERIALS (for two candlesticks)

ball of self-hardening clay about the size of a large apple
*black poster paint
*polymer gloss medium
paintbrush
rolling pin
wax paper
sharp-pointed knife
scissors
small container of water
two 12-inch rulers or two ¼-inch-thick furring strips
barbecue skewer or modeling stick
tracing paper
pencil
tape measure
two candles

INSTRUCTIONS (work both candlesticks simultaneously)

1. With a pencil and tracing paper, trace patterns for base and handle of candlesticks. Cut out the traced patterns. (See tracing instructions, page 26.)

2. With a knife, cut the ball of clay in half. Only half of the clay is needed for each candlestick.

3. Roll the clay into a ball between your two flattened palms.

4. Place clay on wax paper and flatten the ball with the heel of your hand.

5. Roll out the clay with the rolling pin supported at both ends by rulers or furring strips ¼ inch thick. (See Match Holder, Fig. 1, page 76.) The rolled-out clay should be larger than the pattern.

6. Place the candlestick base pattern on the rolled-out clay. Cut away the excess clay with a knife. Roll this remaining clay into a ball and save it for the handle and candle support.

7. Smooth out the edges of the base with moistened fingers.

8. Using the thumb and forefinger of your left hand and the forefinger of your right hand, push and pinch the edges to give them a fluted look. Try to keep the fluting evenly spaced all around the candlestick base.

9. With a knife, cut the remaining clay in half. One half will form the handle and the other half the candle support.

10. Using the tape measure, measure the circumference of the circle. The measurement will tell you how long to make the candle support.

11. To make the candle support, form the clay into a ball and roll it out as above.

12. Cut away the excess clay until you have a rectangle approximately 1½ inches wide by whatever length is needed to hold the candle, plus ¼ inch for overlap.

13. Make this rectangle into the candle support by slightly overlapping the two ends. Smooth out the seam with moistened fingers.

PATTERNS FOR COLONIAL CANDLESTICKS

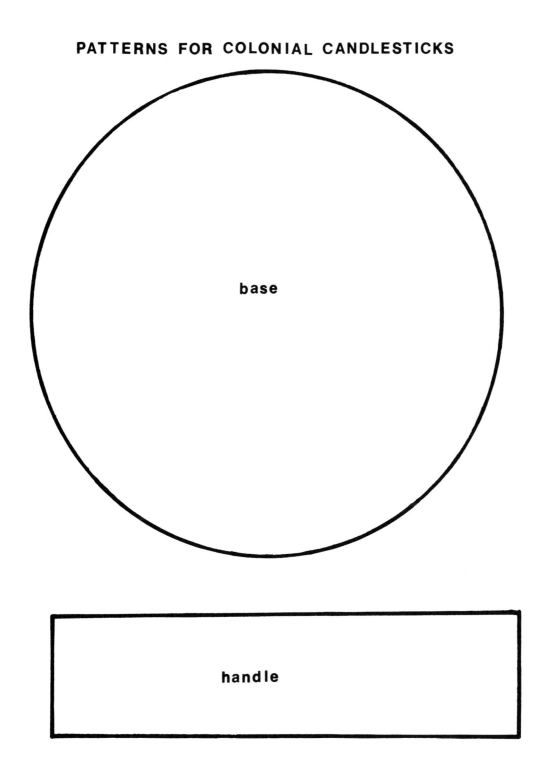

base

handle

14. Join the candle support to the candlestick base by making the bottom edge of the support very wet. To adhere the inside and the outside of the candle support to the base, use the barbecue skewer or modeling stick to join the seams. (Fig. 1) Keep smoothing the seams until the candle support and base become one piece of clay.

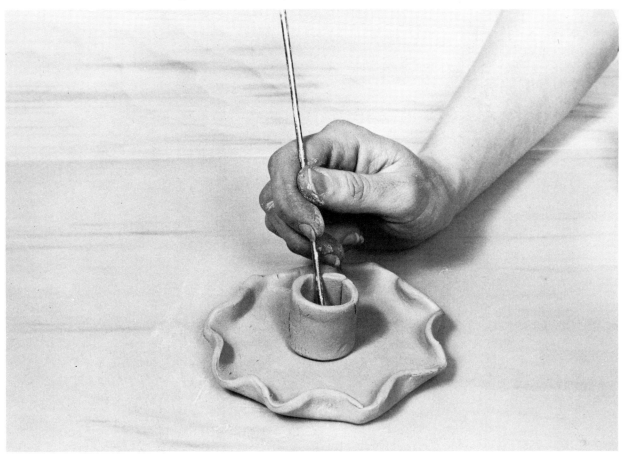

FIGURE 1

15. Roll out the other half of the excess clay as above and place the handle pattern on the rolled-out clay. Cut away the excess clay with a knife. Smooth the edges with moistened fingers.

16. Make this rectangle into the handle by pressing the two ends together.

17. Affix the handle to the base by making the joined ends very wet. Place the handle anywhere on the base about an inch away from the candle support. (Fig. 2)

18. Dip your fingers into water and smooth out the area where you pressed the handle into the base, making sure there are no cracks. Dip your fingers into the water again and smooth out the entire base, candle support, and handle.

19. Keep the pair of candlesticks on wax paper and let them dry for at least three days.

20. Finishing — "Wrought-Iron" Look
    a. Using a clean paintbrush, paint the candlesticks with polymer gloss medium. Let dry for a half-hour.
    b. Using a clean paintbrush, paint the candlesticks with black poster paint. Let dry completely. Paint a second coat over the first and let dry again.
    c. With a clean paintbrush, paint polymer gloss medium over the black paint. Let dry thoroughly. The candlesticks are now ready to receive the candles.

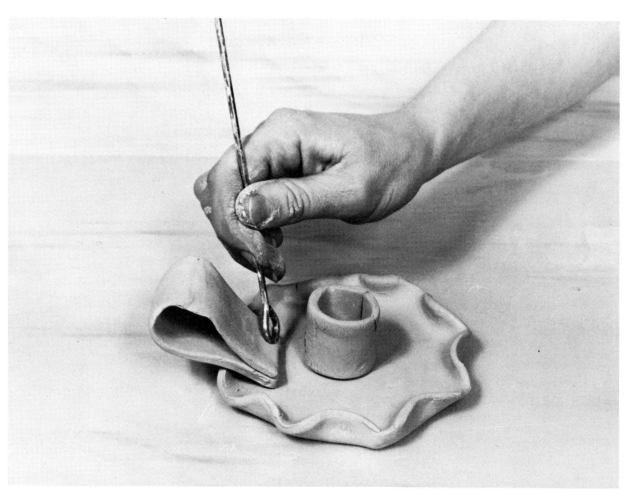

FIGURE 2

CERAMIC AND PAPER BEAD NECKLACE WITH DECOUPAGE PENDANT
(photo, page 158)

MATERIALS FOR PENDANT

self-hardening clay
knife
nail
wax paper
water in small dish
rolling pin
two 12-inch rulers or two wood furring strips 12 by ¼ by 1
    inch (available at lumber dealers)
*poster or tempera paints
paintbrush
gift wrap — one sheet
*polymer gloss medium (decoupage glaze)
pencil
scissors

INSTRUCTIONS FOR PENDANT

1. Cut out a motif from the gift wrap to use as your decoupage appliqué.

2. On wax paper roll out a small ball of clay using a rolling pin and two wood furring strips as illustrated in Match Holder, Fig. 1, page 76. The rolled-out clay must be larger than the pendant pattern.

3. Place the gift wrap appliqué on the rolled-out clay. Cut away excess clay with a knife, allowing a ¼-inch border all around. (Fig. 1) Remove appliqué from clay.

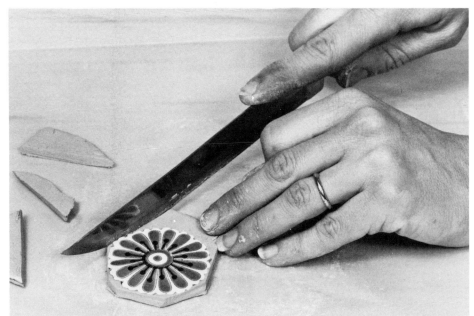

FIGURE 1

4. Smooth out the edges of the clay with moistened fingers.

5. Make a decorative border with the side of a pencil point.

6. Using a nail, make two holes near the top of the clay pendant for lacing that may be strung on later.

7. Allow pendant to dry thoroughly (48 hours).

8. Using a color coordinated to the gift wrap, paint the back of the pendant. Allow to dry (approximately a half-hour).

9. Paint the front and the sides of the pendant. Allow to dry (approximately a half-hour).

10. Brush polymer gloss medium on the back of the decoupage appliqué. Center and press down the appliqué onto the clay pendant. Allow to dry (approximately 15 minutes).

NOTE: *Polymer gloss medium brushes on milky white but dries crystal clear.*

11. Brush polymer gloss medium on the back of the pendant. Allow to dry (approximately 15 minutes).

12. Brush polymer gloss medium over the entire front and sides of the pendant (covering gift wrap) and allow to dry.

13. Repeat steps #11 and 12 until the decoupage appliqué appears embedded in the clay. (We brushed ours with six coats.)

MATERIALS FOR CERAMIC BEADS

self-hardening clay
skewer, knitting needle, or large nail
knife
wax paper
water in a small dish

INSTRUCTIONS FOR CERAMIC BEADS

1. On wax paper, roll out a long (about 12 inches) thin (about ⅜ to ¾-inch) strip of clay with the flattened palms of your hands. (Fig. 1)

2. With a knife, cut the roll of clay into sections of desired bead length (approximately ⅓ to 1¼ inches). (Fig. 2)

3. Thread the beads onto a knitting needle one at a time to make a hole for future stringing. (Fig. 3) If any cracks appear in the bead, moisten the surface with water and smooth with your fingers. To achieve a rough-textured bead, roll bead (on knitting needle) onto a rough surface, such as coarse sandpaper or a vegetable grater.

4. Remove the bead from the knitting needle and set on wax paper to dry.

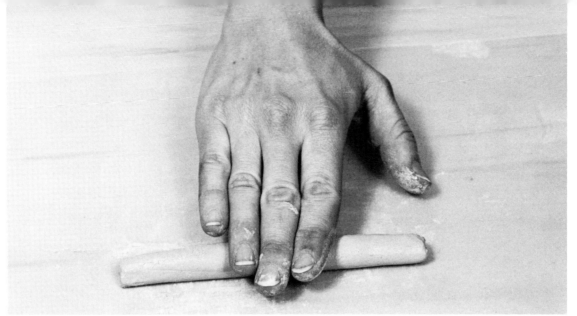

FIGURE 1

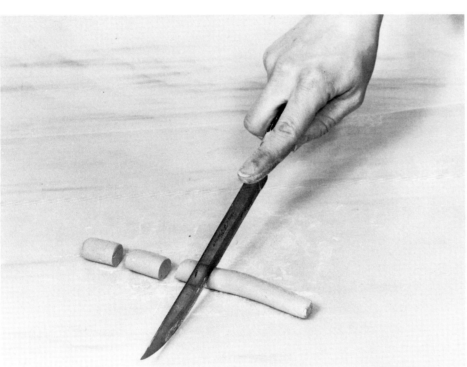

FIGURE 2

FIGURE 3

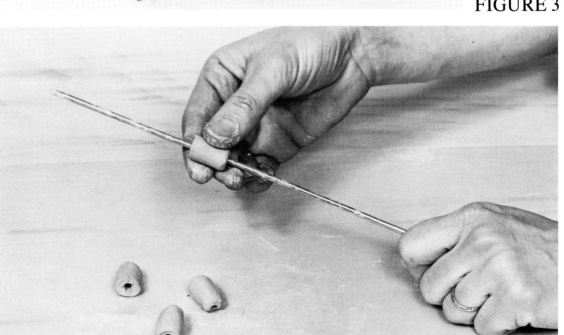

91

FINISHING

The bead finish may match the finish on the pendant as photographed. In this instance, we used green tempera paint, glazed with several coats of polymer gloss medium.

MATERIALS FOR PAPER BEADS

one sheet of gift wrap (left over from pendant)
*white glue
knitting needle or barbecue skewer
*polymer gloss medium
pencil
ruler
paper for tracing pattern
leather thong or lanyard for stringing necklace
paintbrush

INSTRUCTIONS FOR PAPER BEADS

1. With pencil, ruler, and tracing paper, trace and cut out the pattern for the beads. (See tracing instructions, page 26.)

2. Lay the pattern on the gift wrap and trace around it. Repeat this step for each bead desired. Cut out the triangles.

3. Place a knitting needle or a skewer at the wide end of the triangle and roll up as shown. (Fig. 1)

ROLLING UP PAPER ON NEEDLE

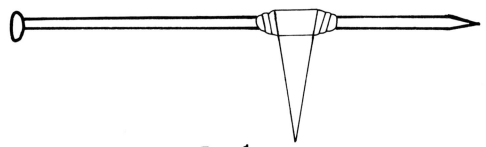

Fig. 1

PAPER BEAD
PATTERN

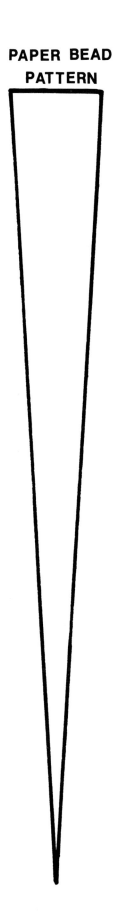

4. Apply a dab of white glue to the point of the triangle and roll to the end.

5. Remove the knitting needle or skewer.

6. Repeat this procedure (steps #3, 4, and 5) until you have made all of your beads.

7. String all the beads onto the knitting needle or skewer and brush the entire surface with polymer gloss medium. Allow to dry.

8. Apply five more coats of polymer gloss medium, allowing drying time between each coat.

Your paper beads are now ready for stringing.

PUTTING YOUR NECKLACE TOGETHER

1. Take the piece of lanyard and cut it in half. Thread each piece of the lanyard through the pendant holes and knot ends.

2. String the beads onto the lanyard, starting first with a ceramic one and alternating a paper bead with a ceramic bead until you have strung half the beads onto one piece of the lanyard.

3. String the other half of the beads onto the second piece of the lanyard in the same way.

Your necklace is now ready for you to wear or to give as a gift.

FREEFORM DESIGN PENDANT
(to Coordinate with
Ceramic and Paper Beads)
(photo, page 158)

MATERIALS

self-hardening clay
thick nail
knife
rolling pin
two 12-inch rulers or two furring strips ¼ inch thick by
    12 inches long (available at lumber dealers)
small paintbrush
*poster paints
brown liquid shoe polish
*polymer gloss medium (decoupage glaze)
one yard of plastic lanyard or leather thong

water
wax paper
scissors
one unpainted ceramic bead
petroleum jelly
tracing paper
pencil

INSTRUCTIONS

1. With pencil and tracing paper trace the pattern for the pendant shape and cut it out. (See tracing instructions, page 26.)

2. On wax paper, roll out a small ball of clay using a rolling pin and two wood furring strips as illustrated in Match Holder, Fig. 1, page 76. The rolled-out clay must be larger than the pendant pattern.

3. Place the paper pattern on the rolled-out clay. Cut away the excess clay with a knife.

4. Now smooth the edges of the clay with moistened fingers.

5. Coat the nail with petroleum jelly. Using this nail, make a long opening through the top of the pendant. The opening has to be wide enough to allow two strips of lanyard to pass through it. Keep the nail in place until the pendant dries. (Fig. 1)

6. The pendant can be left smooth, little bits of clay can be added to make a design, or patterns may be scratched into the clay with a nail.

7. Allow the pendant to dry thoroughly for 48 hours.

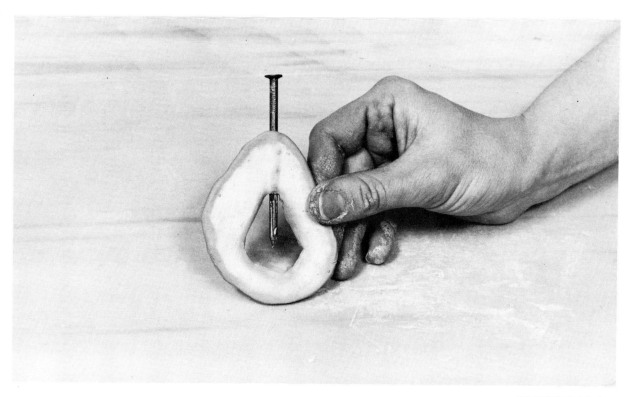

FIGURE 1

8. Brush the back of the pendant with polymer gloss medium. Allow to dry about 15 minutes.

9. Brush the front of the pendant with polymer gloss medium. Allow to dry about 15 minutes.

10. Using a paint color or liquid shoe polish coordinated to the beads, paint the back of the pendant. Allow to dry a half-hour.

11. Paint the front and sides of the pendant. Also allow to dry a half-hour.

12. If you made a raised design on your pendant, paint it with a contrasting color. Allow to dry a half-hour.

13. Now take the unpainted ceramic bead and paint it with a contrasting color also. Allow to dry a half-hour.

14. Brush polymer gloss medium over the front and sides of the pendant. Allow to dry 15 minutes. Brush polymer gloss medium over the back of the pendant and over the bead. Allow both to dry 15 minutes.

15. Take a yard of lanyard and cut it into two 18-inch strips.

16. Thread the two strips through the pendant opening.

17. Take the bead and string it onto the two lanyard strips hanging in the center opening of the pendant. Push the bead up to the bottom of the opening. Make a knot so that the bead will not fall off.

18. String the ceramic and paper beads alternately onto the lanyard. The necklace is now complete.

SHELL MIRROR PLAQUE
(photo, page 158)

MATERIALS

self-hardening clay
variety of three or four types of shells (available from
    general arts and crafts suppliers)
two 12-inch rulers or two 1 by ¼ by 12-inch furring strips
    (available at lumber dealers)
nail or barbecue skewer
3-inch round mirror
*concentrated bonding adhesive
container for mixing concentrated bonding
    adhesive
small cup of water
*polymer gloss medium
paintbrush
knife
rolling pin
wax paper

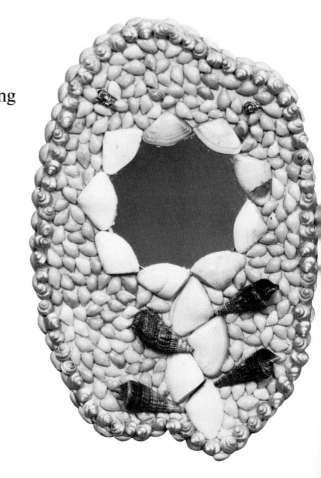

INSTRUCTIONS

1. Roll the clay into a ball between your two flattened palms.

2. Place clay on wax paper and flatten the ball with the heel of your hand.

3. Roll out the clay with the rolling pin supported at both ends by rulers or furring strips ¼ inch thick as illustrated in Match Holder, Fig. 1, p. 76.

4. Using the knife, cut the clay into a freeform shape.

5. Smooth out edges with moistened fingers.

6. Using a nail or skewer, make two holes in the clay for future hanging.

7. Allow plaque to dry for five days, turning it over once each day so that piece can dry evenly.

8. Brush polymer gloss medium on one side; let dry 15 minutes. Brush polymer gloss medium on the other side; let dry for another 15 minutes.

9. In a small container, dilute the concentrated bonding adhesive with three parts water to one part glue.

10. Brush back of mirror with diluted glue and adhere to clay plaque. Let dry for 15 minutes.

11. Arrange one row of shells around the mirror and plan the remainder of your design. Glue shells to clay plaque using the diluted glue solution. Let dry for an hour.

12. Brush the remainder of the diluted glue over the entire plaque except for the mirror. Let dry overnight.

13. Brush polymer gloss medium over the entire plaque except for the mirror. Let dry for an hour and give the plaque a second coat.

NEEDLEPOINT PURSE ACCESSORIES

The needlepoint purse accessories described in this book are worked on a translucent white plastic canvas made by Columbia-Minerva called Fashion-Ease. This canvas, which is available in 10½ by 13½-inch sheets, is sold at yarn stores. We highly recommend it for the purse accessories because of its special characteristics:

seven holes to the inch (large enough for large-eyed
    needles to pass through easily)

pliable

easy to cut with household scissors

holds its shape, requiring no blocking

smooth edges do not unravel, eliminating the need to fold
    edges for finishing

designs may be drawn on with waterproof markers (these
    markers have an odor)

One sheet of this canvas will be more than sufficient to make one eyeglass case, one picture holder, and one key chain.

NOTE: If you have difficulty locating a source for this canvas, write to Columbia-Minerva Company, 295 Fifth Avenue, New York, New York 10016, (212-685-2907) for shopping information.

HALF-CROSS STITCH

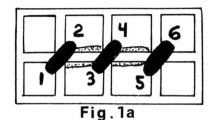

Fig. 1a

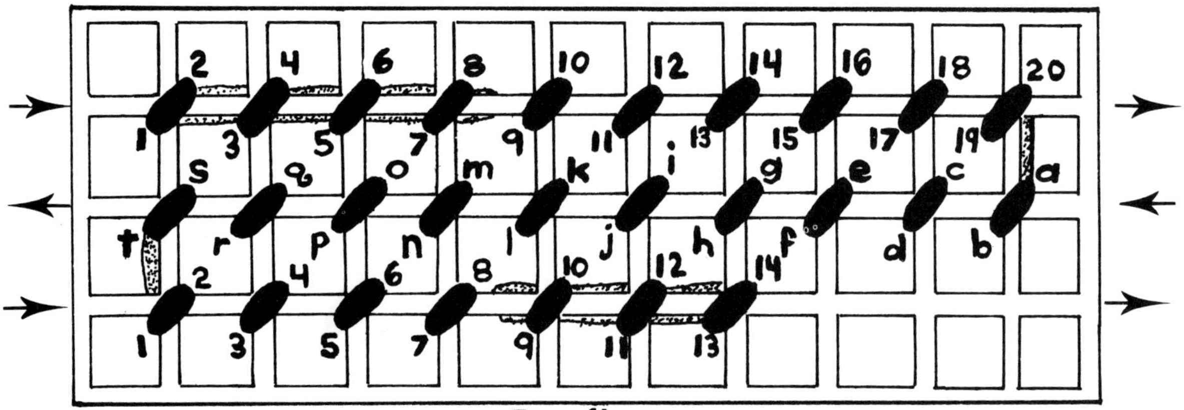

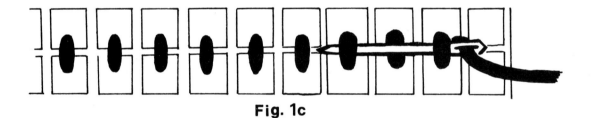

Fig. 1b

Fig. 1c

FIGURE 1a

    Cut yarn to 24-inch length. Do not knot the end of the yarn. The needle comes up at 1 and down at 2. Catching the end of your yarn in the back of the next few stitches, continue coming up through the canvas at odd numbers and down through the canvas at even numbers.

FIGURE 1b

    To continue to the next row, come up through the canvas at a, down at b, up at c, etc. (Some people prefer to turn the canvas upside down and continue to work the second row.) Proceed to the third row in a similar manner.

FIGURE 1c

    When you come to the end of the yarn, work the needle alternately over and under a few stitches on the back of the canvas.

101

BINDING STITCH

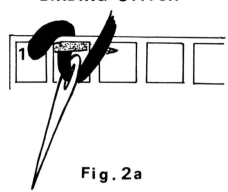

Fig. 2a

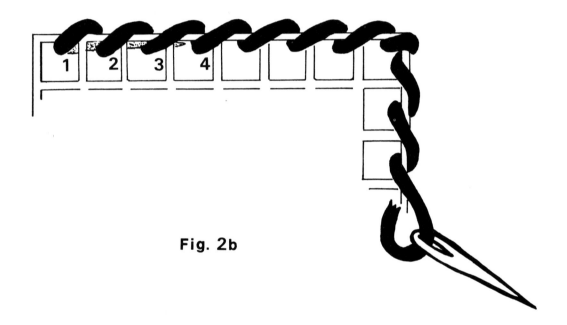

Fig. 2b

FIGURE 2a

    Cut yarn to 24-inch length. Do not knot end. Bind off the edge of the canvas by coming up once through each successive hole in the canvas, catching the yarn end in the back of the first few stitches.

FIGURE 2b

    To turn a corner on the canvas, work through the corner hole twice and continue. NOTE: The binding stitch may be used to join two pieces of canvas — lay one piece of canvas on top of the other, lining up the holes exactly. Work through the two pieces of canvas simultaneously as you would one piece of canvas.

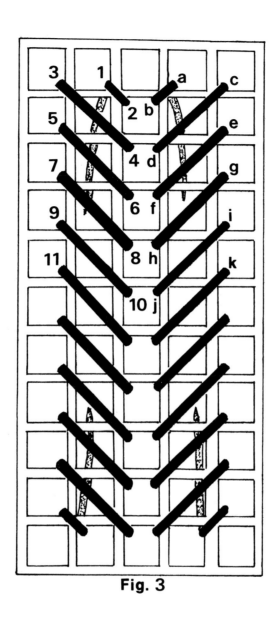

Fig. 3

FIGURE 3

Cut yarn to 24-inch length. Do not knot the end of the yarn. The needle comes up at 1 and down at 2. Catching the end of your yarn in the back of the next few stitches, continue coming up through the canvas at odd numbers and down through the canvas at even numbers. In contrasting yarn, work the pattern in reverse, coming up through the canvas at a, down through the canvas at b, and up through canvas at c, etc. End off by inserting the needle under the stitches on the back.

103

SCOTTISH DIAGONAL STITCH
REVERSE DIAGONAL STITCH

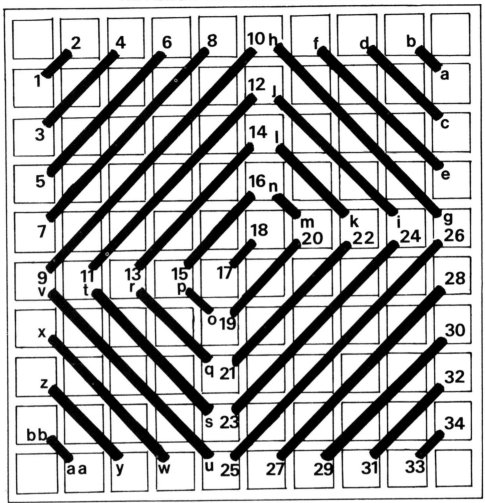

Fig. 4

FIGURE 4

Cut yarn to 30-inch length. Do not knot the end of the yarn. The needle comes up at 1 and down at 2. Catching the end of your yarn in the back of the next few stitches, continue coming up through the canvas at odd numbers and down through the canvas at even numbers — up at 33 and down at 34 — and end off by inserting the needle under the stitches on the back.

Cut yarn to 24-inch length. Do not knot the end of the yarn. With contrasting color, work the pattern in the reverse direction, coming up through the canvas at a, down through the canvas at b, up at c, etc. On lower left-hand square, come up at aa and down at bb. End off by inserting the needle under the stitches on the back.

104

EASY-TO-DO NEEDLEPOINT EYEGLASS CASE
(photo, page 159)

MATERIALS

plastic canvas, 7 holes to the inch (Columbia-Minerva
    Fashion-Ease)
choice of #16, 17, or 18 chenille needle
ombre (multicolored) Orlon yarn in knitting worsted
    weight
scissors

INSTRUCTIONS

1. Cut the plastic canvas so that there are 43 holes across and
41 holes down.

2. Thread needle with 24-inch length of ombre yarn. (See
needle-threading instructions, page 28.)

3. Following the instructions for half–cross stitch (page 101),
work the entire canvas in this stitch, using ombre yarn. The
yarn will create its own colorful pattern.

4. Following the instructions for the binding stitch (page 102),
bind the top edge of the eyeglass case (43 stitches).

5. Find the center bottom hole (#22) of the eyeglass case and
work the binding stitch in this hole.

6. Fold the eyeglass case. Continue the binding stitch
through both layers of canvas. Complete the bottom and side.

7. Finish off by working needle through last several binding
stitches and clip exposed end.

NOTE: To make coordinating key chain and picture holder, follow the
instructions for the Checkerboard Needlepoint Key Chain and Picture Holder (pages 108 and 111), substituting ombre yarn and half–
cross stitch throughout.

STITCH PATTERN FOR CHECKERBOARD NEEDLEPOINT EYEGLASS CASE

top

bottom

106

color key

 color A

 color B

 color C

CHECKERBOARD NEEDLEPOINT EYEGLASS CASE
(photo, page 159)

MATERIALS

plastic canvas, 7 holes to the inch (Columbia-Minerva
   Fashion-Ease)
choice of #16, 17, or 18 chenille needle
three colors of Orlon yarn in knitting worsted weight
scissors

INSTRUCTIONS

1. Cut the plastic canvas so that there are 43 holes across and
41 holes down.

2. Thread needle with a 24-inch length of yarn. (See needle-
threading instructions, page 28.)

3. Refer to the enlarged checkerboard eyeglass case pattern, page 106.

4. Following the stitch instructions for the half–cross stitch, page 101, work a two-row border around entire canvas in color A.

5. Following the stitch instructions for the stem stitch, page 103, work stem stitch in colors B and C as indicated on the pattern chart.

6. Follow the stitch instructions for the Scottish diagonal stitch and reverse diagonal stitch, page 104, in colors B and C, as indicated on the pattern chart.

7. Complete the eyeglass case according to steps #4 to 6 of the Easy-to-Do Needlepoint Eyeglass Case (page 105), using yarn color A.

CHECKERBOARD NEEDLEPOINT KEY CHAIN
(photo, page 159)

MATERIALS

plastic canvas, 7 holes to the inch (Columbia-Minerva Fashion-Ease)
choice of #16, 17, or 18 chenille needle
three colors of Orlon yarn in knitting worsted weight
key chain finding (available from Tandy Corporation)
scissors
ruler

STITCH
PATTERN FOR CHECKERBOARD
NEEDLEPOINT KEY CHAIN

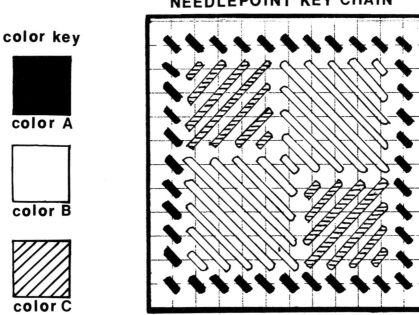

color key

color A

color B

color C

INSTRUCTIONS

1. Cut the plastic canvas to approximately 2 by 2 inches. Make sure that there are 12 holes across and 12 holes down.

2. Thread needle with a 24-inch length of yarn. (See needle-threading instructions, page 28.)

3. See pattern above and refer to stitch instructions on pages 101 and 104.

4. Work a one-row border in half–cross stitch completely around the square using color A.

5. Work Scottish diagonal stitch in color B.

6. Work reverse Scottish diagonal stitch in color C.

7. Make a second piece of work exactly the same way.

8. With wrong sides facing, use the binding stitch to join the two finished squares. Use color A and double yarn. Start in the center of any side. Work around to the third corner.

ASSEMBLY OF KEY CHAIN

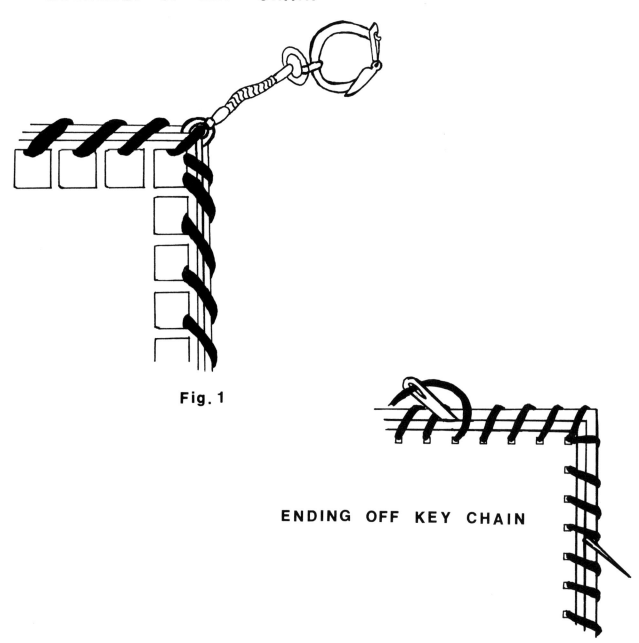

Fig. 1

ENDING OFF KEY CHAIN

Fig. 2

9. Insert the small ring of the key chain finding between the two canvases. Continue binding stitch through the canvases and the ring. (Fig. 1)

10. Continue binding stitch to starting point.

11. Insert needle between canvases. (Fig. 2.) Pull needle through. Clip end of yarn.

CHECKERBOARD NEEDLEPOINT PICTURE HOLDER
(photo, page 159)

MATERIALS

plastic canvas, 7 holes to the inch (Columbia-Minerva
    Fashion-Ease)
choice of #16, 17, or 18 chenille needle
three colors of Orlon yarn in knitting worsted weight
acetate pockets to hold photos (available at variety stores
    or by mail order from Tandy Corporation)
wing insert binder (also available from Tandy
    Corporation)
masking tape
scissors
tracing paper
pencil

INSTRUCTIONS

1. Using pencil and tracing paper, trace the four pattern
pieces and cut out. (See tracing instructions, page 26.)

2. Lay the tracing paper patterns on the plastic canvas and
hold them in place with masking tape. Cut out the patterns
on the plastic canvas.

3. Refer to the enlarged picture holder pattern on page 113.

**PATTERNS FOR CANVAS
PARTS OF NEEDLEPOINT PICTURE HOLDER**

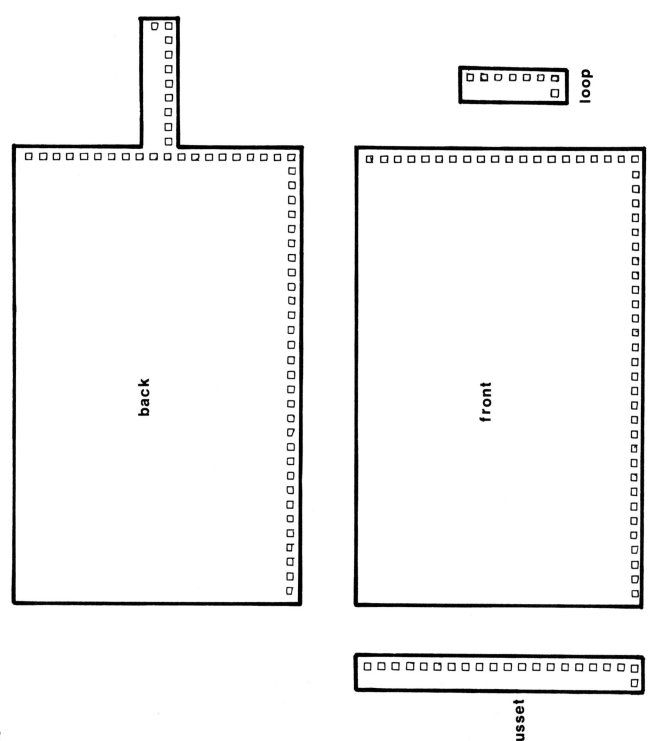

4. Work the front as follows:
   a) Following the stitch instructions for the half–cross stitch (page 101) and with color-B yarn, work a three-row border all around the four sides of the canvas.
   b) Using the half–cross stitch and color-A yarn, make a two-row border all around the four sides within the above border.

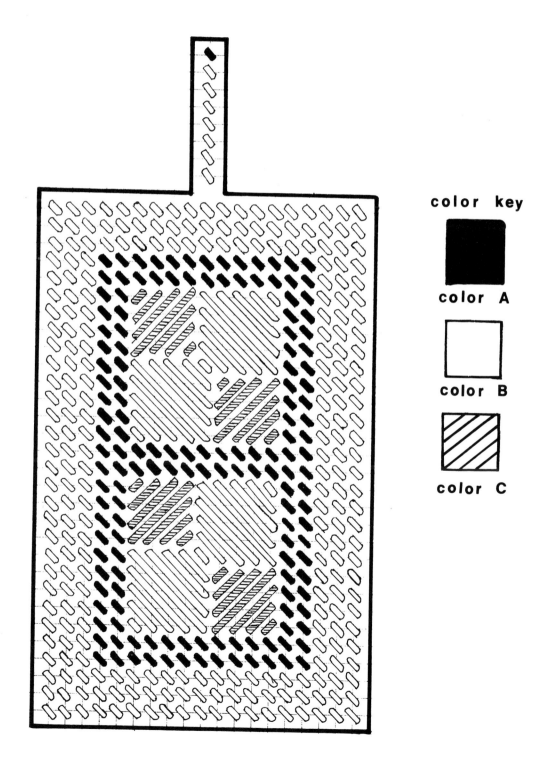

STITCH PATTERN FOR CHECKERBOARD
NEEDLEPOINT PICTURE HOLDER

color key

color A

color B

color C

113

PICTURE HOLDER ASSEMBLY

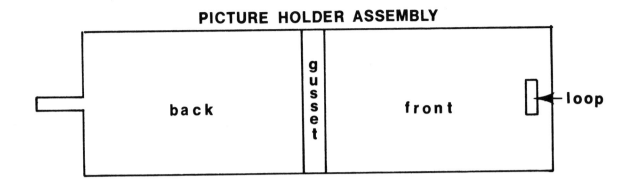

Fig. 1

c) Using the half–cross stitch and color-A yarn, make a two-row vertical border going down the center of the remaining blank canvas.
d) Follow the stitch instructions for the Scottish diagonal stitch and reverse diagonal stitch (page 104) in colors B and C to fill in the remaining canvas.

5. To work the back, follow the instructions for the front. For the extension flap work the center row in the half–cross stitch and the edges in binding stitch (page 102) in color-B yarn, except for the last row, which is to be worked in the same manner in color-A yarn. (When the extension is tucked into the loop on the front, the designs will match.)

6. Work the gusset in two rows of the half–cross stitch in color-B yarn.

7. To make the loop, work the center row in the half–cross stitch and the edges in the binding stitch in color-B yarn.

8. Assemble the picture holder as follows:
a) Lay the loop vertically, centered one row in from the right-hand edge. Sew the top and bottom edges of the loop to the front in this position. (Fig. 1)
b) Lay the pieces right side up on the worktable, from left to right: the back, the gusset, the front.
c) Using the binding stitch and color-C yarn, attach the back, the gusset, and the front together.

WOOD PROJECTS

If you have never worked with wood, we hope you will be enticed by our projects and give them a try. These projects require no previous experience.

Lumberyards usually provide a customer lumber-cutting service. The scrap or waste lumber is either given away or sold at a very nominal cost. The wood projects we have described require such scrap lumber. Ask the folks at the lumberyard to keep you in mind and save you some scraps. Check in at the lumberyard regularly to gather your loot; they will probably be willing to cut the wood to proper size for you even if they give you the wood for free. By the way, lumberyards usually have scraps of all kinds of building materials — Homasote, particle board, paneling, Masonite, peg boards, dowels, moldings, etc. Think up some clever projects to utilize such materials. Let us know how you are doing!

NOTE: The actual lumber dimensions do not measure to the name specifications of the standard lumber sizes. For example, 1 by 6-inch lumber really measures ¾ by 5½ inches. Our project instructions refer to standard lumber sizes.

DECOUPAGE PLAQUE
(photo, page 160)

MATERIALS

newspaper
sandpaper (medium, fine)
sanding block (optional)
stiff-bristled brush
picture from a greeting card, gift wrap, or a print
piece of solid wood or plywood up to 1 inch thick, cut to
    dimensions that will allow an even border around the
    picture
scissors
hammer
nails (various sizes)
screwdriver
*polymer gloss medium
*acrylic wood stain or brown latex paint (diluted)
*white glue
stirrer for mixing paint
rag
lint-free cloth
1-inch brush
wax paper
wallpaper seam roller, brayer, or the back of a spoon
choice of saw-tooth hanger, wire and screw eyes, decora-
    tive hook and eye, wall mount strips

FIGURE 1

FIGURE 2

INSTRUCTIONS

PREPARING THE BOARD

1. Cover the work area with newspaper.

2. Sand the rough edges on the wooden board with medium, then fine, sandpaper. (See sanding instructions, page 22.)

3. Remove the sawdust from the board with the stiff-bristled brush.

DISTRESSING THE BOARD (to give it an antique quality)

1. Make "age cracks" by scoring the surface of the wood plaque with the corner of the tip of a screwdriver. Make the scores varying distances apart, lengths, and depths, always in the direction of the grain of the wood. (Fig. 1)

2. Make "worm holes" by hammering various size nails into the wood about ⅛ inch deep, then withdrawing the nails. Cluster several nail holes for a natural effect. These "worm holes" are effective toward the edge of the board. Remember, the decoupage picture will cover the center of the board, so

FIGURE 3

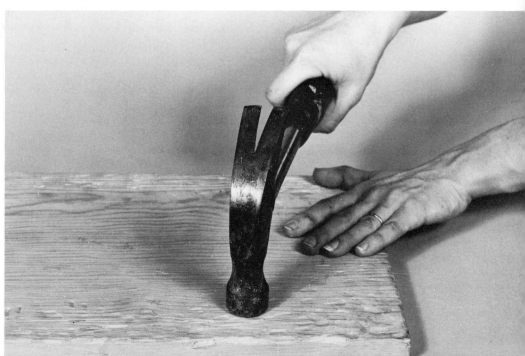

don't bother making worm holes that won't show. Avoid making too symmetrical or regular a pattern of worm holes that will appear artificial. (Fig. 2)

3. Make dents in the board by hammering it at odd intervals. (Fig. 3)

STAINING THE BOARD

Acrylic wood stain is preferred over an oil stain because of its easy water clean-up and quick-drying properties. If acrylic wood stain is unavailable, brown latex paint may be substituted. Thin the paint with water (in about equal parts) until enough water has been added to give the paint a translucent quality. When the diluted paint is applied to the wood, the wood grain shows through. A rag is preferred for applying the stain or paint evenly, but a brush will be satisfactory. (Read painting instructions, page 25.)

1. Cover the newspaper with a layer of wax paper to prevent sticking.

2. Apply the stain to the edges of the board. Then apply the stain to the top surface, using long strokes the full length of the board, going in the direction of the grain of the wood.

3. Inspect the board from all angles to make sure you didn't leave any "holidays" (spots not covered with stain). Let the stain soak into the wood for about five minutes.

4. Using a clean, dry, lint-free rag, wipe over the entire surface of the stained board, using long strokes with the grain of the wood, removing excess stain. The graining of the wood, the worm holes, and the age cracks will appear darker than the rest of the board. Allow the board to dry for an hour.

5. If you want the color of the wood to be darker or intensified, repeat the staining procedure.

PREPARING AND APPLYING THE PICTURE

We recommend that you select a picture from a greeting card, a print, or gift wrap. Although magazines provide a source of attractive pictures, they are difficult to use because the matter on the reverse side bleeds through unless the picture is first treated with a spray sealer. Also, magazine pictures tend to wrinkle and bubble easily because the paper on which they are printed is so thin.

1. With scissors, trim the excess border around the picture. Gently tear the remaining border down while holding the picture firmly in your other hand. This method of tearing produces a feathered edge that does not show a jagged white line. Do not attempt to tear in a straight line. An irregular edge is more natural. (Fig. 4)

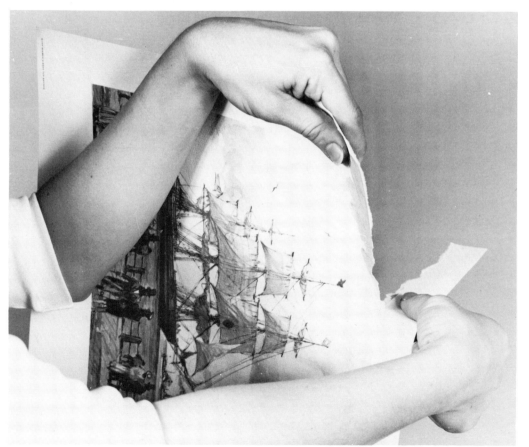

FIGURE 4

2. With a 1-inch brush, apply a thin, even coat of white glue on the entire back of the picture. Make sure there are no "holidays" that will cause a bubbling on the finished plaque. If you are gluing a large picture, make sure the glue is still wet before you affix the picture to the board. If necessary, 119

sprinkle drops of water over the dried areas and spread the water with your fingers so that the back of the picture is completely wet.

3. Turn over the picture and carefully center it on the board (do not press the picture in place until you are satisfied that it is well centered on the board).

4. Press the picture firmly to the board, using a small brayer or the back of a spoon, starting with the center and working toward the edges. (Fig. 5) If any part of the edge lifts away from the board, apply extra white glue under the edge and press it down again. Allow one hour to dry. This drying time is *essential* to prevent the picture from bubbling.

FIGURE 5

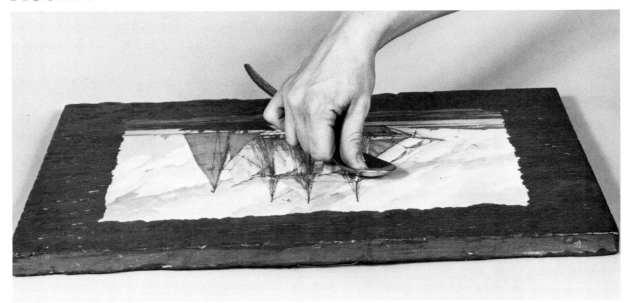

5. Going with the grain of the wood, brush over the entire surface of the board and the picture with polymer gloss medium, using long, even strokes. Allow to dry for an hour. Repeat this step until the picture appears embedded in the board. NOTE: *Polymer gloss medium goes on milky white but dries crystal clear.*

6. Use wall mount strips, picture hanging kits (wire and screw eyes), saw-tooth hanger, or decorative hooks and rings to mount the finished decoupage.

VALET
(photo, page 160)

MATERIALS

1 by 12-inch lumber, 2½ feet long
plastic desk organizer approximately 9 by 11 inches
    (available in variety stores)
two café curtain hooks to accommodate wood dowel
12-inch wood dowel, ½ inch wide
*Weldbond adhesive
tracing paper
pencil
scraps of felt and material
4 by 4-inch mirror
self-stick letters
sandpaper (medium, fine)
*acrylic wood stain
paintbrush
straight pins or masking tape
newspaper
wax paper
pressure-sensitive metallic braid (available through Hazel
    Pearson's Handicrafts, P.O. Box 519, 4128 Temple City
    Boulevard, Rosemead, California 91770 — 213-443-
    6136, or Lee Wards)

marking pen (broad tip)
saw-tooth picture hangers with nails
crosscut saw
screwdriver
awl
hammer
two small corner braces with small screws

INSTRUCTIONS (Reminder: read carpentry instructions, page 18.)

1. With crosscut saw, cut the lumber as follows:
   16-inch-long piece for the back of the valet
   9-inch-long piece for the shelf of the valet

2. With sandpaper (medium, then fine), sand any rough edges.

3. Apply a little dab of Weldbond adhesive to the back of one of the curtain rod hooks. Place this hook along the long side of the organizer, about ½-inch in from the edge. Affix the second hook in the same manner to the other edge of the organizer. Allow the adhesive to dry for approximately an hour.

4. Apply a little Weldbond adhesive to the inside of the curtain hooks where the wood dowel will rest. Set the dowel in place on the curtain hooks. Allow the adhesive to dry for approximately an hour.

5. Spread newspaper on a table and place wax paper on top of it. Put your pieces of wood on the wax paper and stain one side. Allow stain to dry for approximately three hours. Turn pieces of wood over and stain the other sides as well as all of the edges. Again allow stain to dry for approximately three hours.

6. Mount two saw-tooth hangers, one at each side, 1 inch from top of valet, to prevent the valet from swaying when mounted on the wall.

7. With tracing paper and pencil, trace and cut out pattern pieces #1 (oval), 2, 3, 5, 6, and 7. (See tracing instructions, page 26.)

FELT APPLIQUÉ PATTERNS FOR VALET

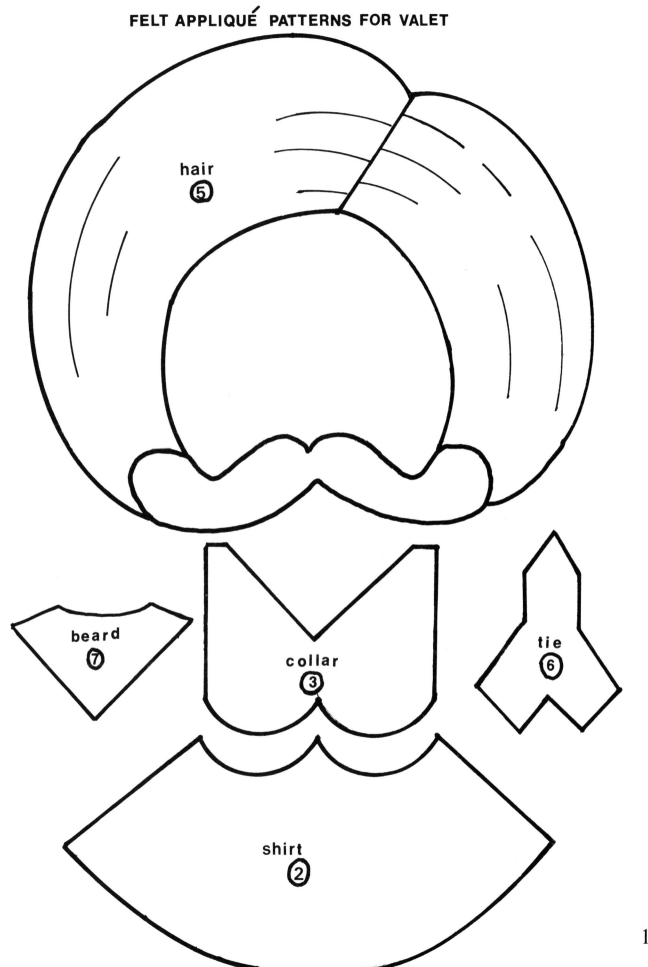

hair ⑤

beard ⑦

collar ③

tie ⑥

shirt ②

123

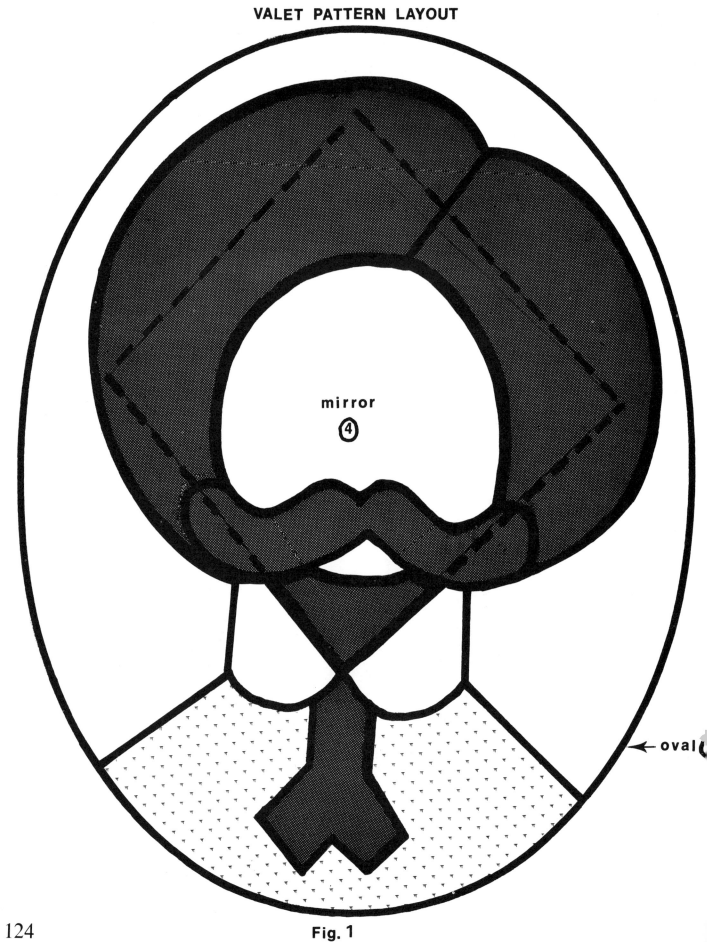

mirror

④

← oval

124　　　　　　　Fig. 1

8. Lay the patterns on the appropriate pieces of material, pin or tape them down, and cut out.

9. Place all the pieces of material on the 12 by 16-inch piece of wood and center them according to the pattern layout. (Fig. 1) Using Weldbond adhesive, glue down pieces #1, 2, and 3 in numerical order. Glue the mirror (#4) so that a corner of it fits into the angle of the collar (#3). Glue the hair and mustache (#5) over the mirror. Glue down pattern pieces #6 and 7.

10. Place letters to spell ''Man of the Year'' around the top of the oval felt piece, making sure your letters and words are evenly spaced. Peel backing off self-stick letters and press into place.

11. Peel backing from self-adhesive trim and press into place around oval felt piece. If self-adhesive trim is not available, use regular material trim and glue into place with Weldbond adhesive.

FIGURE 2

125

12. With the marking pen sketch hairline and mustache lines onto felt piece #5 according to pattern piece.

13. To attach the shelf to the back, spread a thin line of glue along the bottom front edge of the 12 by 16-inch piece of wood. Press the 9 by 12-inch piece against it. Lay these two pieces on their sides and lean the can of stain against them. (This helps the adhesive to bond.) Allow to dry for approximately an hour. (Fig. 2)

14. Position corner braces to reinforce joints on back and bottom of the valet 2 inches from the outside edges. Mark screw positions onto wood in pencil. Start holes by hammering awl on pencil marks. Reposition braces and tighten screws with screwdriver.

15. Apply some Weldbond adhesive to the underside of the plastic organizer in each of the four corners. Press into place on the 9 by 12-inch piece of wood. Allow glue to dry for approximately a half-hour.

TABLETOP BOOKSTAND
(photo, page 160)

MATERIALS

*wood glue
crosscut saw
two C clamps
sandpaper
    (coarse, medium, fine)
sanding block
hammer
1½-inch brads
    (about a dozen)
countersink
masking tape
awl or nail
tracing paper
pencil

yardstick

12-inch ruler

choice of finishes, materials, and tools needed to apply the
    desired finish — acrylic stain, latex paint, decoupage

1 by 10-inch pine board, 18 inches long

1 by 2-inch furring strip, 2 feet long

two hinges, 1½ by ⅞ inches, and 8 screws

INSTRUCTIONS

MEASURING AND SAWING

1. With a pencil and yardstick measure and mark off the 1 by
10 by 18-inch board as follows: one 11¼-inch length for the
main piece; one 5½-inch length for the easel back.

2. Measure and mark off on the furring strip two 11¼-inch
lengths for the book ledge.

3. Using a crosscut saw (and C clamps to support the board
on the worktable — optional), cut the four pieces of lumber
to size.

PATTERN FOR CURVE ON TOP OF BOOKSTAND

4. With a pencil and tracing paper, trace and cut out the
curve pattern that will be used for both the top of the main
piece and for one of the furring strips.

5. Lay the curve pattern on the right side of the top of the
main piece. Trace around the pattern with a pencil. Repeat
this step on the left side, reversing the pattern. (Fig. 1)

6. Repeat step #5 on the furring strip.

FIGURE 1

7. Using a coping saw and C clamps to support the board on the worktable, cut the curve as follows: start in the center of the curve by cutting straight down to the traced line at a right angle to the wood. Withdraw the saw and cut on the traced curved line beginning at one end and working toward the center cut. Work the same way from the opposite end.

8. Repeat step #7 on the furring strip.

9. Using sandpaper mounted on a sanding block (coarse, then medium, then fine), sand smooth all the rough edges.

BOOKSTAND ASSEMBLING INSTRUCTIONS

1. To mark off the placement of the hinges on the piece, with a ruler and pencil measure down 3¾ inches from the middle of the two highest points of the curves. Connect these two points with a straight line. Measure and mark 1¾ inches in from the two side edges along this line. (Fig. 2)

2. Place each hinge on the pencil line 1¾ inches in from the side edge. Use the 1¾-inch mark you made as a guide. The pencil line should be in the middle of the screw holes on the hinge plate. With a pencil, trace the four screw holes.

3. Using a hammer and awl, make starter holes centered in the outline of the four traced screw holes.

PLACING HINGES ON BACK OF BOOKSTAND

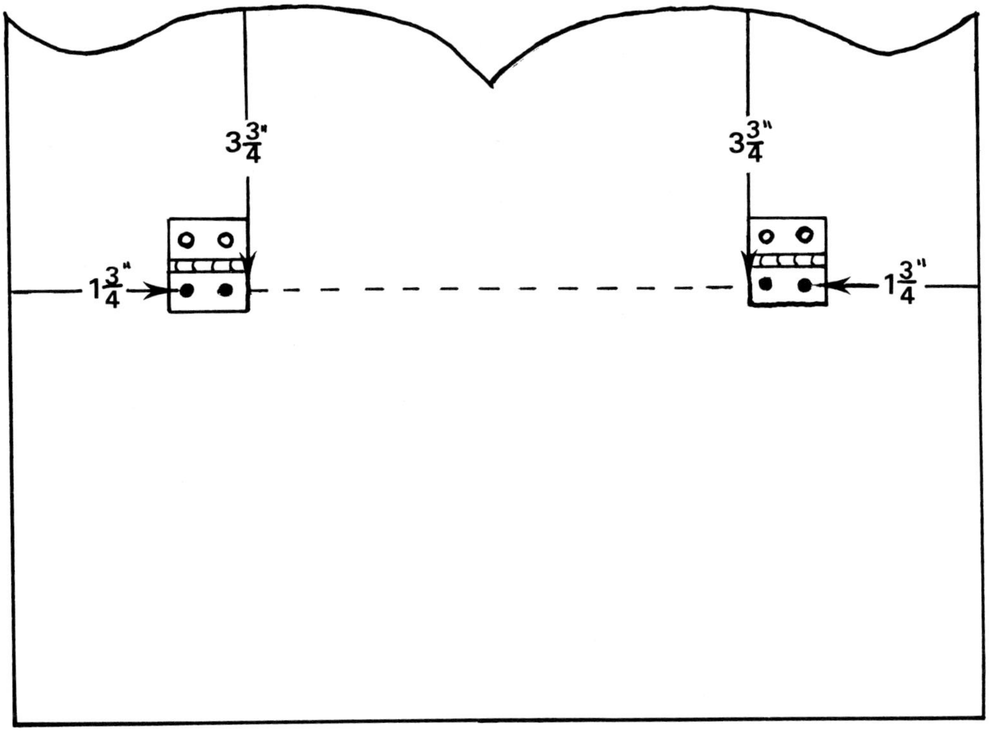

Fig. 2

4. Line up each hinge on the screw starter holes. Remember that when the other plate of the hinge is attached to the easel back, the hinge should be underneath the easel back. With a screwdriver, attach all four screws to the main piece.

5. To affix the hinges to the easel back, center the top of the easel back over the detached hinge plates and with a pencil trace the four screw holes.

6. With a hammer and awl, make starter holes centered in the outline of the four traced screw holes.

7. Screw the hinges onto the easel back with a screwdriver.

8. Attach the furring strip ledge as follows:
   a. Spread wood glue over the long narrow side edge of the plain furring strip. Adhere the furring strip to the front bottom of the main piece. Line up the edges evenly.
   b. Support the joint with masking tape.
   c. Spread wood glue over the other long narrow edge of the attached furring strip. Attach the second furring strip to the first so that the curved edge faces upward and forms a ledge. Support this joint with masking tape.

d. Let the glue dry for twenty-four hours.

e. Reinforce the joint edges of the ledge by hammering 1¼-inch brads along the back of the main piece and along the front of the curved furring strip. HINT: Alternate the positions of the brads so that the wood will not split. (Fig. 3)

9. Countersink the brads on the front-curved furring strip. (See Fig. 11, page 24.) Fill in the countersink holes with wood glue. Let the glue dry for three hours and then sand until smooth.

FINISHING

1. The bookstand can be painted with latex paint, (see painting instructions, page 25), stained with acrylic stain, (see staining techniques on the finishing chart, page 36), or decoupaged (see decoupage instructions, page 119).

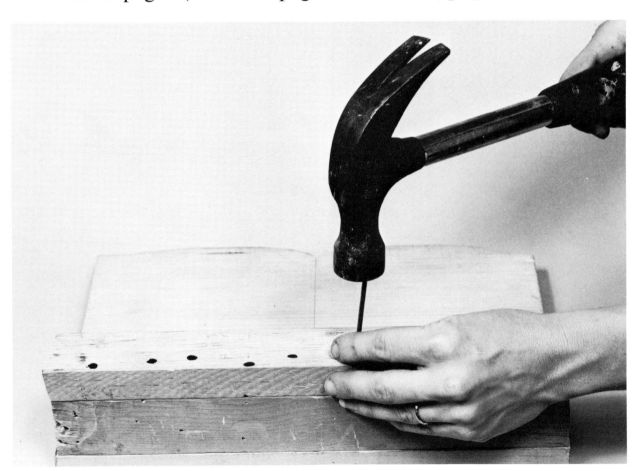

WOOD AND NEEDLECRAFT PROJECTS

Each of the projects in this section combines simple carpentry with needlecraft. The projects utilize basic tools that most people have in their homes and the carpentry needs only small pieces of lumber.

The needlecraft part of the projects includes weaving and rug hooking.

We have combined two different craft media to create beautiful home accessories.

CONTEMPORARY WOVEN PILLOW
(photo, page 160)

MATERIALS FOR LOOM

furring strip 1 by 2 inches by 8 feet
*wood glue
seventy brads 1¼ inches long
hammer
saw
pencil
yardstick
sandpaper
masking tape

INSTRUCTIONS FOR LOOM (Reminder: read over carpentry instructions, page 18.)

1. Cut the furring strip into four pieces, each 16 inches long. Sand all the rough edges.

2. Using a yardstick as a guide, draw a pencil line lengthwise down the center of two of the furring strips. Starting 1¼ inches from the end, mark dots on this line at ½-inch intervals on both strips. There will be 28 dots on each furring strip. (Fig. 1)

FRAME ASSEMBLY

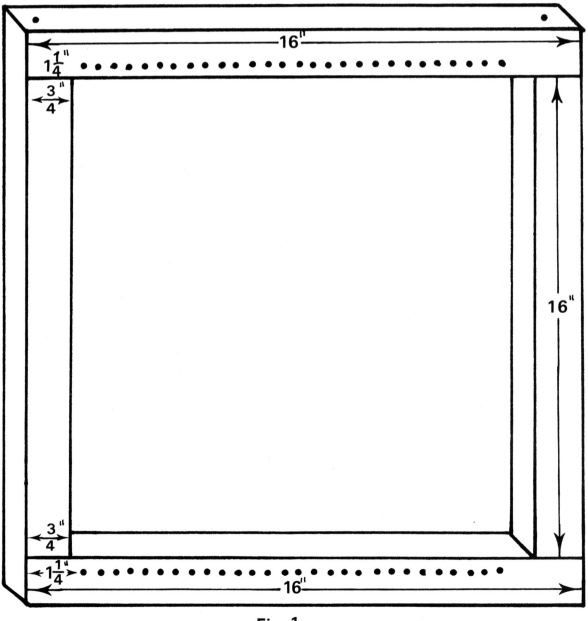

Fig. 1

3. Hammer a brad ¾ inch deep into each dot marked on the two lengths of furring strips, making sure that the brads do not penetrate to the other side of the strips. These two furring strips will be the top and bottom of the weaving frame.

4. Glue together all four lengths of furring strips into a rectangle with butt joints. (Fig. 1)

5. Apply several pieces of masking tape over the joints to hold them in place as the glue dries. Remove the tape when the glue has dried thoroughly (overnight).

6. Reinforce the corners with brads.

MATERIALS FOR CONTEMPORARY WOVEN PILLOW

Three 70-yard skeins of rug yarn in coordinating colors
weaving needle (long needle with large eye made
   expressly for weaving) or #13 tapestry needle

scissors
16 by 16-inch piece of fabric for pillow backing
straight pins
ruler
pencil
1½ by 6-inch piece of cardboard for making fringes
stuffing for pillow
crochet hook H
sewing needle
coordinated thread for sewing pillow together

INSTRUCTIONS FOR CONTEMPORARY WOVEN PILLOW

STRINGING THE WARP (see photograph on page 131
for numbering boards)

Choose one color of yarn for the warp. Wind this yarn around
the brads as follows:

Make a knot around nail 1. Go up to 2, around 4, and down to
3; back to 1, up to 2, and around to 6 (covering 3 nails); down
to 5, around 7, and up to 8; around 10, down to 9, around
to 11; and continue stringing in this manner until you reach
the end. (Fig. 2) To tie off stringing, go around 55, up to 56,
back over to 54, and make a double knot around 54. (Fig. 2)
Support your end warps (A and BB) by looping and tying yarn
around these warps and the sides of your frame. (Fig. 2)
These loops will prevent your weaving from pulling
inward. You may slide these loops up as you work. Cut off
the loops when you have finished your weaving project.

NOTE: The brads in Fig. 2 appear to be positioned in pairs and closer
together than ½ inch in order to accurately illustrate the finished look
of the warp. We emphasize that the brads should be placed ½ inch
apart when you build your frame.

WEAVING THE PATTERN (consult your pattern chart, Fig. 3,
while working)

NOTE: See Fig. 6 for weaving the weft.

1. Now you are ready to begin weaving. Choose another
color and cut off a workable length (about 36 inches). Thread

start

Fig. 2

your needle with one end of this yarn and with the other end tie a weaver's knot (Fig. 5) around warp A, which is a double warp. Proceed to weave by placing the needle under warp B, over warp C, under warp D, etc., across the row. (Fig. 6)

Weave loosely enough to prevent the warps from pulling toward the center. After each new row, push your work down toward the bottom of the loom.

135

PATTERN CHART FOR WOVEN PILLOW

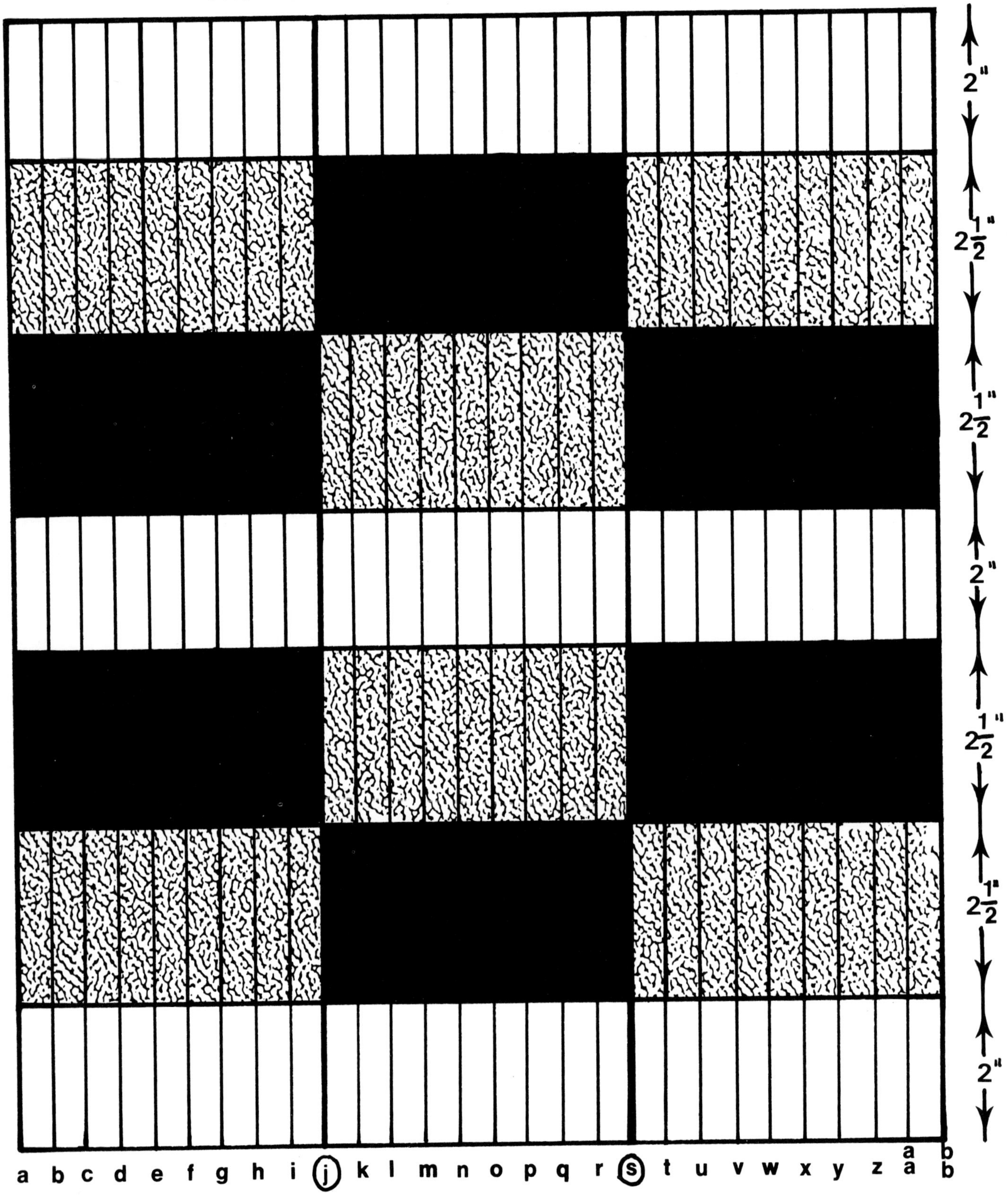

Fig. 3

WEAVER'S KNOT

Fig. 5

WEAVING THE WEFT

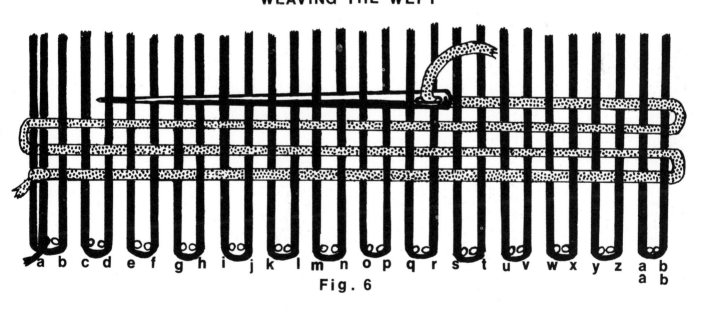

a b c d e f g h i j k l m n o p q r s t u v w x y z a b
a b
Fig. 6

2. Take a length of the second color and tie it to warp A. Thread the needle. This color will be worked over warps A through J in the manner described above. Work this color up 2½ inches. Cut yarn off at the end. Leave a 6-inch end hanging, which will be woven in at warp J as you work the next step.

137

3. Cut a length of the third color and knot it around warp J between the first and second rows of your previous work in second color. (Fig. 7) Work across ten warps to warp S. Continue weaving between warps J and S for 2½ inches, always weaving in between your previous work at warp J. Clip a 6-inch end and leave it hanging. Knot the ends to your future work.

**HOW TO
CHANGE COLOR ON WARP**

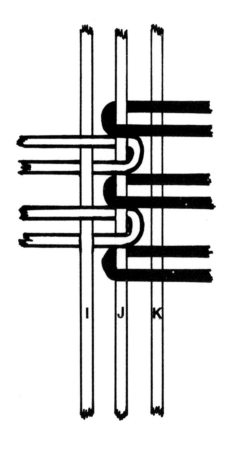

Fig. 7

4. Cut a length of the second color and tie it around warp S. Weave across the remaining warps to warp BB for 2½ inches in the same manner as step #3.

5. Following the pattern design, continue weaving in the manner described. (Fig. 3)

MAKING THE PILLOW

1. When the weaving is finished, remove it from the loom by lifting the warps from the brads one at a time. (Do not worry about your work unraveling — the warps will form a bound edge.)

2. With right sides facing, center the weaving on the fabric for pillow backing. Pin three sides together. Using a back stitch (Fig. 8) and doubled sewing thread and needle, sew the three sides together close to the edge of the weaving. Cut excess material away, leaving 1 inch all around as a seam allowance.

Fig. 8 BACK STITCH

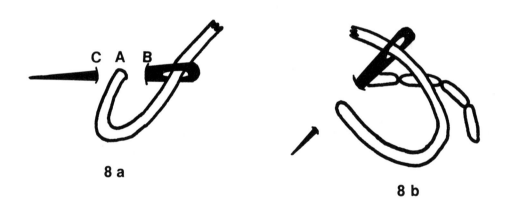

8 a

8 b

FIGURE 8a
    Work from right to left. Bring the needle up through the fabric at A. Insert the needle through the fabric a short distance to the right of A at point B and bring the needle up through the fabric to the left of point A at point C. Points B and C are equidistant from point A.
FIGURE 8b
    Continue by inserting the needle through the fabric in the same hole at the left end of the previous stitch and bringing the needle through the fabric the same distance as the first stitch made. The back stitch is used to make outlines.

3. Turn pillow right side out and stuff.

4. Tuck in 1-inch seam allowance on the fabric pillow backing and pin fourth side closed.

5. Using a whip stitch (Fig. 9), sew the fourth side of the pillow closed.

WHIP STITCH

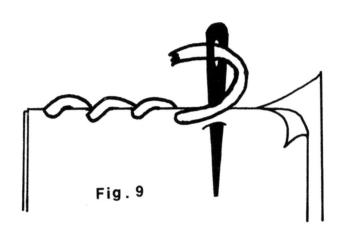

Fig. 9

FIGURE 9

The whip stitch is used to join fabrics. Draw the needle through both fabrics close to the edge. To make small, almost invisible, stitches work the stitches close together.

MAKING THE FRINGE

1. Cut your piece of cardboard to 1½ by 6 inches.

2. Choose the color you want for your fringe and wrap the yarn around the 1½-inch width of the cardboard. After you have wound the yarn around the cardboard a number of times, take the scissors and clip along the bottom edge. (Fig. 10)

3. Insert the crochet hook into a loop, take a piece of fringe yarn, fold it in half over the crochet hook (Fig. 11a), pull yarn through the loop (Fig. 11b), catch both ends of the yarn with hook of crochet needle, and pull through loop (Fig. 11c). One fringe has been made. (Fig. 11d) Continue to cut yarn fringes and crochet them onto pillow as described above, placing one fringe into each loop. Fringe all four edges.

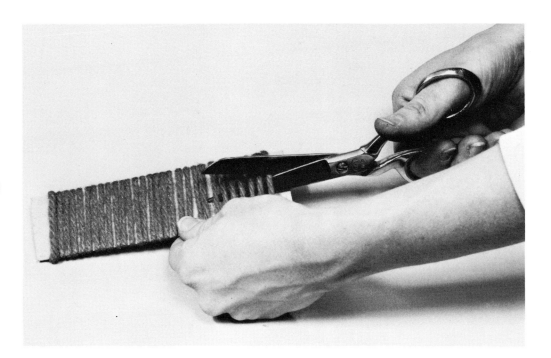

FIGURE 10

Fig. 11   HOW TO MAKE A FRINGE

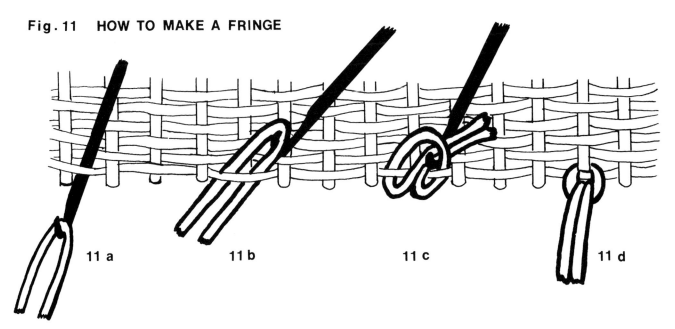

11 a   11 b   11 c   11 d

FIGURE 11

    A. Fold a 3-inch length of yarn in half, forming a loop. Insert the crochet hook through the edge cross strand of the woven pillow. Catch the yarn loop in the crochet hook.

    B. Pull the yarn loop through the edge cross strand about ¾ inch.

    C. Catch the two ends of the yarn in the crochet hook and pull them through the loop.

    D. Pull the yarn ends with your fingers. The fringe is finished. Trim ends if desired.

RUG-HOOKED MAGAZINE RACK
(photo, page 160)

MATERIALS FOR FRAME

1 by 8-inch pine board, 3½ feet long
½-inch dowel, 3 fect long
two drawer pulls with machine screw fittings
8 flat head wood screws, size 6 by 1½ inches
hand drill
drill bit, size 5/32 inch
sandpaper (coarse, medium, fine)
sanding block
two C clamps, 3 inches
crosscut saw
coping saw (optional)
screwdriver
awl
hammer
yardstick
pencil

*latex paint or acrylic stain
1-inch paintbrush
stirrer to mix paint
finishing nail
four thumbtacks
newspaper

INSTRUCTIONS FOR FRAME (Reminder: read over carpentry instructions, page 18.)

MEASURING AND SAWING (Fig. 1)

1. Using a pencil and yardstick, measure and mark off on the pine board two 12-inch lengths for the sides of the frame.

2. Measure and mark off on the pine board one 15-inch length for the bottom of the frame.

3. Using a crosscut saw (and C clamps to support the board to the worktable — optional), cut the three pieces of the frame to size.

4. With a pencil and yardstick, measure and mark off two 15-inch lengths of the ½-inch dowel.

5. With a coping saw (or crosscut saw), cut the dowels to size. These dowels will support the rug canvas on the frame.

6. Using sandpaper mounted on a sanding block (coarse, then medium, then fine), sand smooth all the rough edges on the side pieces, bottom, and dowel ends.

INSTRUCTIONS FOR FRAME ASSEMBLY

1. With a pencil, trace the outline of the end of the dowel in a corner of both side pieces (as close to the edges of the side pieces as possible). (Fig. 2)

2. Trace the outline of the end of a dowel in the opposite corner along the 8-inch edge of both side pieces.

143

Fig. 1   MAGAZINE RACK FRAME PARTS

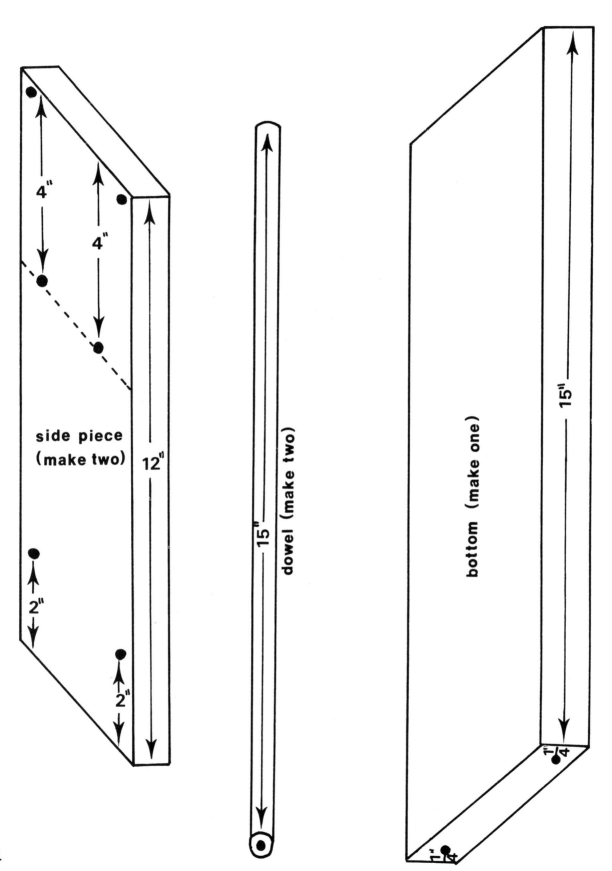

side piece (make two)

4"

4"

2"

2"

12"

dowel (make two)

15"

bottom (make one)

15"

$\frac{1}{4}$"

$\frac{1}{4}$"

FIGURE 2

3. With a hammer and awl, make starter holes in the centers of the four dowel outlines on the side pieces.

4. Using C clamps, support the side pieces to the worktable, positioning the boards so that the holes to be drilled extend beyond the worktable (to avoid drilling holes through the worktable).

5. With a hand drill and a 5/32-inch bit, drill these four starter holes clear through the boards. These holes are at the top of the side pieces and will be used later to connect the dowels.

6. With a pencil and yardstick, measure and mark off the side pieces 2 inches from the bottom and ¼ inch from the side edges. (Fig. 1) Follow steps #3, 4, and 5 to drill holes at these four marks. These holes will be used to fasten the bottom of the magazine rack.

7. To position the handles, measure and mark off a line 4 inches from the tops of the side pieces. Center the handles on these lines.

8. Trace around the handle machine screw fittings onto the side pieces.

9. Follow steps #3, 4, and 5 to drill holes on these four markings. These holes will be used to fasten the handles after the project is completed.

10. Clamp an end of a dowel tightly in a C clamp. Use a second C clamp to attach the first to the edge of the worktable. The clamped dowel end should be facing upward vertically. (See Fig. 13, page 25.)

11. Using a hammer and awl, make a starter hole in the end of a dowel. Using the hand drill, drill a hole ½ inch deep into the end of the dowel. Repeat steps #10 and 11 at the other end of this dowel and at both ends of the second dowel.

12. Using a screwdriver and four 6 by 1½-inch screws, attach the two dowels securely to the tops of the side pieces. (Fig. 3)

FIGURE 3

13. Position the bottom piece between the side pieces 2 inches from the bottom. Using a hammer and finishing nail, make starter holes on the bottom piece by hammering the nail through the drilled holes on the bottom of the side pieces. Withdraw the finishing nail after making the starter holes.

14. Remove the bottom piece and clamp it to the worktable with C clamps. Using the hand drill, drill the four starter holes ½ inch deep.

15. Return the bottom piece to its proper position between the side pieces, lining up the drilled holes. With a screwdriver and four 6 by 1½-inch screws, attach the bottom piece to the side pieces. (Fig. 3)

16. To finish the magazine rack frame, follow the finishing instructions for the Tabletop Bookstand on page 130.

17. Using a screwdriver, attach the handles to the outer sides of the magazine rack.

MATERIALS FOR RUG HOOKING

½ yard of rug canvas, 36 inches wide
seven 70-yard skeins of rug yarn:
    background color (A) — 3 skeins; main flower color (B) — 2 skeins
    flower centers color (C) — 1 skein; leaf color (D) — 1 skein
latchet hook
scissors
white heavy-duty sewing thread
chenille needle, choice of #20–24
yardstick
*acrylic paint (any vivid color)
#1 artist paintbrush
tracing paper
pencil
cardboard: 6 by 1½ inches for winding and cutting yarn
    for background, flowers, leaves, and stems; 6 by 2 inches
    for winding and cutting yarn for flower centers
masking tape, 1½ inches wide
felt-tip marker
newspaper

INSTRUCTIONS FOR RUG HOOKING

PREPARING THE RUG CANVAS

1. Lay newspaper over the worktable.

2. With a yardstick and felt-tip marker, measure and mark off side seam allowances on the canvas 1½ inches deep along the 36-inch-long edges.

3. Measure and mark off the two front panels and bottom on the rug canvas 14½ inches from the 18-inch edges. Within the seam allowances, the front panels measure 15 by 14½ inches and the bottom panel measures 7 by 15 inches. (Fig. 4)

4. Apply the masking tape to the 18-inch length of the cut edges of the rug canvas so that ¾ inch of the width of the masking tape is on the front. Fold over the remaining ¾ inch to the back of the canvas. This masking tape–bound edge will prevent unraveling and protect your hands from scratches.

5. With pencil and tracing paper, trace the patterns for the flowers, leaves, and stems. With scissors, cut out the pattern pieces.

6. Lay the pattern pieces on one front section of the canvas, positioning the flowers no higher than 5½ inches from the top selvage. (Fig. 4) To attach the pattern pieces to the canvas use small pieces of masking tape, rolled up sticky side out, attached to the wrong side of the pattern pieces.

7. With a #1 artist paintbrush and acrylic paint thinned to a fluid consistency, outline the patterns onto the rug canvas. Allow the paint to dry.

8. Remove the pattern pieces and place them on the other front section of the canvas. (Fig. 4) The pattern is reversed but it will appear right side up when the canvas is positioned on the frame. Outline the patterns on the canvas with acrylic paint. Remove the paper patterns after the painted outlines have dried.

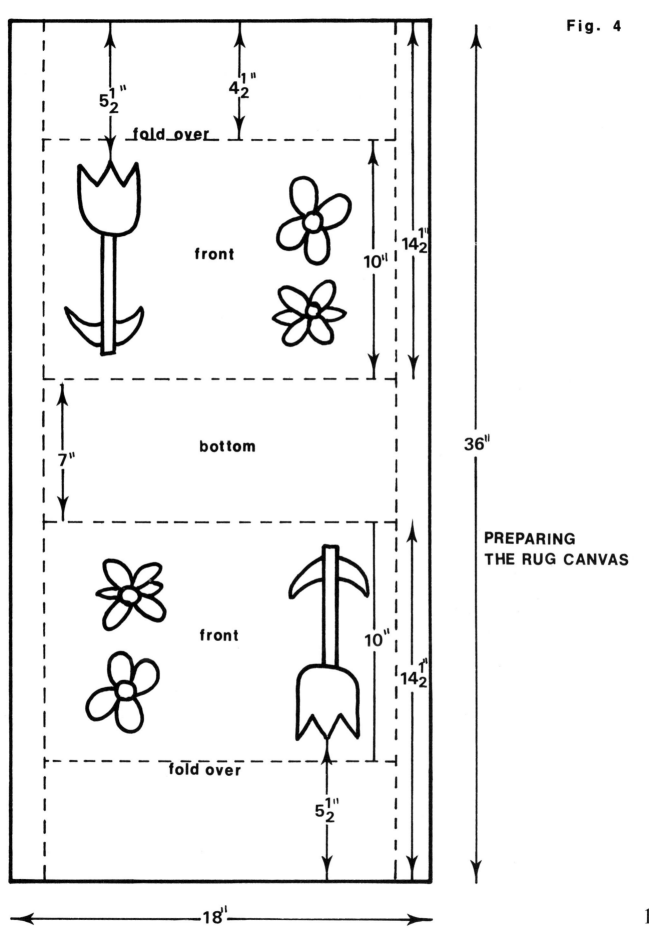

Fig. 4

$5\frac{1}{2}''$ $4\frac{1}{2}''$

fold over

front

$10''$ $14\frac{1}{2}''$

$7''$

bottom

$36''$

PREPARING
THE RUG CANVAS

front

$10''$ $14\frac{1}{2}''$

fold over

$5\frac{1}{2}''$

$18''$

149

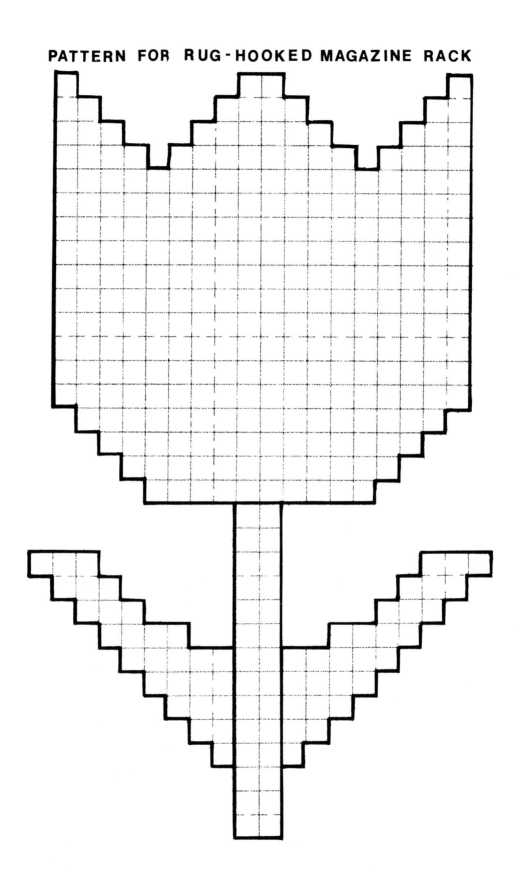

PATTERNS FOR RUG-HOOKED MAGAZINE RACK

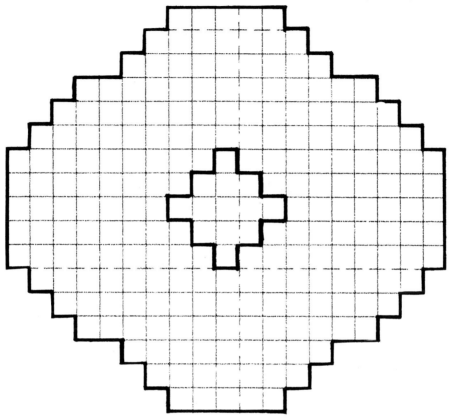

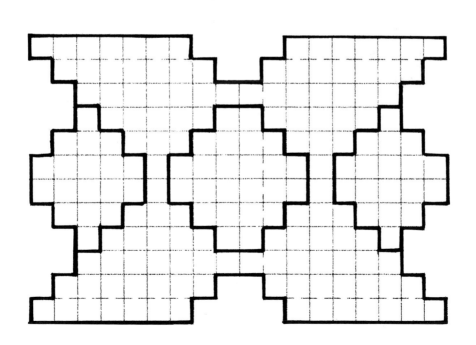

CUTTING THE RUG YARN

1. Rug yarn colors A, B, and D will be cut as follows: Wrap the yarn around the 1¼-inch-wide cardboard so that the yarn does not overlap. Cut the yarn through the middle. (See photo, page 141.) The yarn lengths will measure 2½ inches.

2. Rug yarn color C will be cut in the same manner on the 2-inch-wide cardboard. The yarn lengths will measure 4 inches.

LATCHET-HOOKING THE CANVAS

1. With latchet open, work the hook under one cross strand of the rug canvas. (Fig. 5)

2. Loop a length of cut rug yarn under the base of the hook and above the handle. (Fig. 6)

3. Place both ends (make the lengths even) of the yarn into the open hook. (Fig. 7)

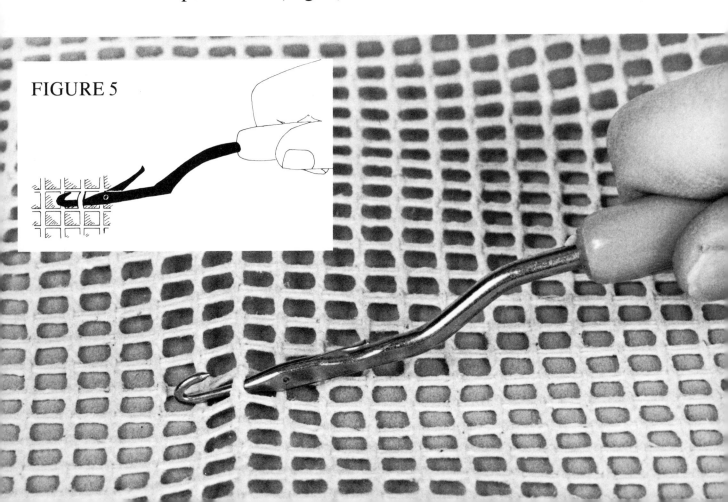

FIGURE 5

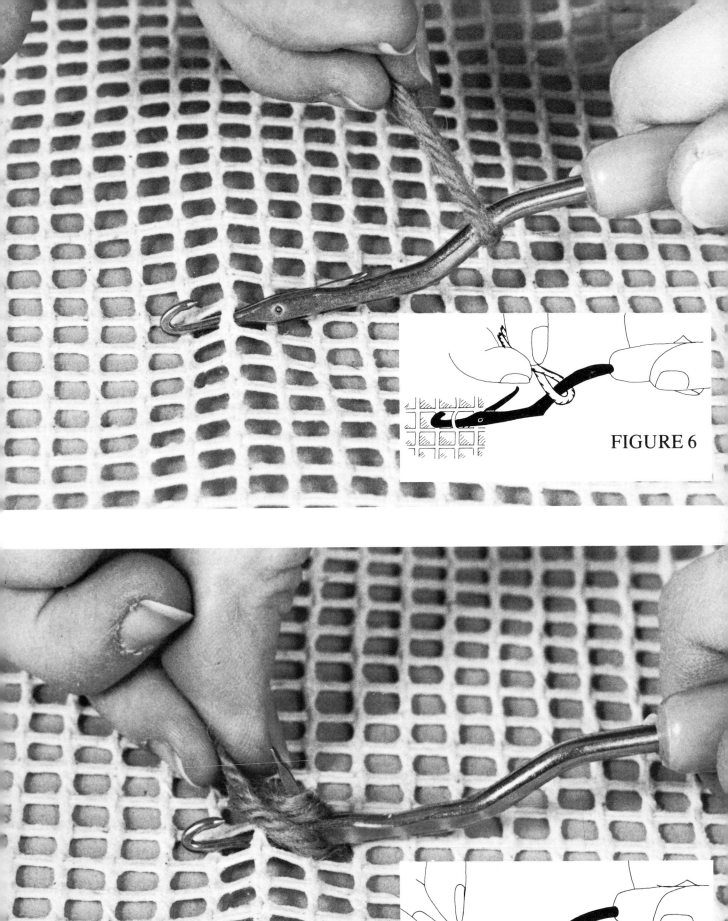

FIGURE 6

FIGURE 7

FIGURE 8

FIGURE 9

4. Tug the hook toward you, bringing the yarn ends through the loop under the base of the hook. (Fig. 8)

5. With your fingers, grasp and tug the yarn ends to tighten the knot. (Fig. 9)

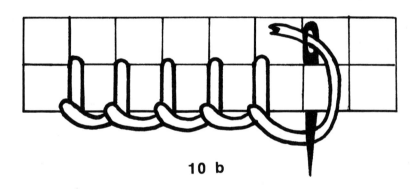

Fig. 10 BLANKET STITCH

10 a

10 b

FIGURE 10a
    On the wrong side of the canvas, bring the needle up through both layers of canvas at the left edge to be bound at A. Hold the thread down with your thumb. Catch the cross threads of both layers of canvas at B (one canvas hole above and to the right of A). Bring the needle up at C (one hole to the right of A), catching the yarn at the canvas edge below the point of the needle.
FIGURE 10b
    A series of blanket stitches is illustrated, binding the turned edge of the canvas.

Always hold the canvas in the same direction so that the knots face in the same direction. Work the canvas from the bottom up (across the rows) so that your hand rests on the yarn rather than on the rough canvas. Turn over the canvas to the reverse side periodically to be sure that you do not leave any spaces undone. Do not work any rug hooking on the side seam allowances or on the bottom panel. If you wish, you may work the bottom panel in the half–cross stitch, page 101. However, this bottom panel will not be visible when the canvas is mounted on the magazine rack frame.

FINISHING AND MOUNTING THE RUG-HOOKED CANVAS

1. Fold side seam allowances to the back of the canvas. Using white heavy-duty thread and a chenille needle, sew the side seam allowances to the hooked canvas. Use the blanket stitch (Fig. 10), and catch one strand of the hooked canvas with each stitch. Space the stitches ¼ inch apart (one stitch in each hole on the rug canvas).

2. To make dowel casings, fold down the top selvages of the rug canvas to a depth of 4 inches. Pin and sew the selvage edges to the hooked canvas using the blanket stitch in the same manner as above.

3. Slip the dowels through the dowel casings on the rug hooking.

4. Attach one dowel to the magazine rack frame with 6 by 1½-inch screws and a screwdriver.

5. Bring the hooked canvas underneath the bottom of the magazine rack frame.

6. Attach the second dowel to the frame.

Your magazine rack is ready to receive your favorite magazines.

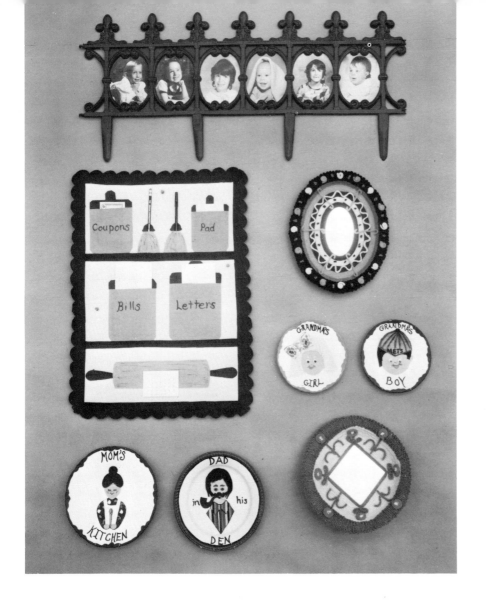

158

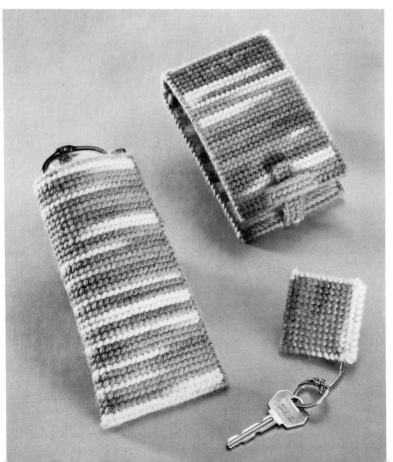

Photograph by Henry Tofte, Lumenphore, Ltd.

Chapter 5

MAIL-ORDER SUPPLIES

This brief listing of mail-order arts and crafts supply companies provides ample sources for obtaining the craft materials required for the projects described in this book. The entries are not intended as an endorsement of these companies.

ARTS AND CRAFTS SUPPLIERS

American Handicrafts Company
1011 Foch
Fort Worth, Texas 76107
(This address is the national office.
Write for local distributors.)
phone: 817-335-4161

Dick Blick Company
Box 1267
Galesburg, Illinois 61401
phone: 309-343-6181

Boin Arts and Crafts Company
87 Morris Street
Morristown, New Jersey 07960
phone: 201-539-0600

Economy Handicrafts
50-21 69th Street
Woodside, New York 11377
phone: 212-426-1600

Hortoncraft (Horton Handicraft
   Company, Incorporated)
P.O. Box 330
Farmington, Connecticut 06032
phone: 203-747-5551

J & A Handy-Crafts, Incorporated
210 Front Street
Hempstead, New York 11550
phone: 516-292-1220

Magnus Craft Materials, Incorporated
304-8 Cliff Lane
Cliffside Park, New Jersey 07010
phone: 201-945-8866-7

Sax Crafts
P.O. Box 2002
Milwaukee, Wisconsin 53202
phone: 414-272-4900

Tandy Corporation
2727 West 7th Street
Fort Worth, Texas 79901
phone: 817-335-2551

Triarco Arts and Crafts
(*See below for address nearest you*)

Cavalier Handicrafts Division
Richmond Leather Division
1839 West Broad Street
Richmond, Virginia 23220
phone: 804-359-1345

Creative Hands Division
4146 Library Road
Pittsburgh, Pennsylvania 15234
phone: 412-563-6344

Delco Craft Division
1000 Troy Court
Troy, Michigan 48084
phone: 313-585-4080

Gager's Handicraft Division
3516 Beltline Boulevard
St. Louis Park, Minnesota 55416
phone: 612-929-2696

J. C. Larson Division
52 West Carpenter Avenue
Wheeling, Illinois 60090
phone: 312-338-7220

Triarco Arts and Crafts
5737 38th Avenue North
St. Petersburg, Florida 33710
phone: 813-344-5711

Triarco Arts and Crafts
220 Carillon Tower East
13601 Preston Road
Dallas, Texas 75240
phone: 214-661-3036

Vanguard Crafts
2915 Avenue J
Brooklyn, New York 11210
phone: 212-377-5188

ARTIST MATERIALS SUPPLIERS

Bee-Ko Company Inc.
155 East 44th Street
New York, New York 10017
phone: 212-682-4224

Bergen Arts & Crafts
P.O. Box 381–H6
Marblehead, Massachusetts 01945
phone: 617-631-8440

Irving Berlin, Inc.
14 East 37th Street
New York, New York 10016
phone: 212-532-3600

Dick Blick Company
Box 1267
Galesburg, Illinois 61401
phone: 309-343-6181

Arthur Brown and Brother, Inc.
2 West 46th Street
New York, New York 10036
phone: 212-575-5555

Cloder Corporation
49-51 Ann Street
New York, New York 10038
phone: 212-962-1600

Macmillan Arts and Crafts
9520 Baltimore Avenue
College Park, Maryland 20740
phone: 301-441-2420

New York Central Supply Company
62 Third Avenue
New York, New York 10003
phone: 212-473-7705

S & S Arts & Crafts
Norwich Avenue
Colchester, Connecticut 06415
phone: 203-537-2325

Sax Arts and Crafts
P.O. Box 2002
Milwaukee, Wisconsin 53201
phone: 414-272-4900

NEEDLECRAFT SUPPLIERS

Herrschners, Incorporated
Hoover Road
Stevens Point, Wisconsin 54481
phone: 715-341-0560

Merribee
2904 West Lancaster
Fort Worth, Texas 76101
phone: 817-332-3983

Lee Wards
P.O. Box 206
Elgin, Illinois 60120
phone: 312-697-3800

Wyco Products
814 Greenwood Avenue
Jenkintown, Pennsylvania 19046
phone: 215-884-6881
(yarn, needlepoint, and
   rug canvas only)

Two worthwhile reference books that will aid you in pursuing crafts are the following:
1) *The National Guide to Craft Supplies* by Judith Glassman, published in 1975 by Van Nostrand Reinhold Company, 450 West 33rd Street, New York, New York 10001, $6.95 soft cover — a complete mail-order shopping guide giving detailed shopping information for all listings.
2) *Craft Sources — The Ultimate Catalog for Craftspeople* by Paul Colin and Deborah Lippman, published in 1975 by M. Evans & Company, 216 East 49th Street, New York, New York 10017, $12.50 hard cover, $5.95 soft cover — a comprehensive craft guide that gives detailed descriptions of available books, magazines, organizations, supplies, and schools.

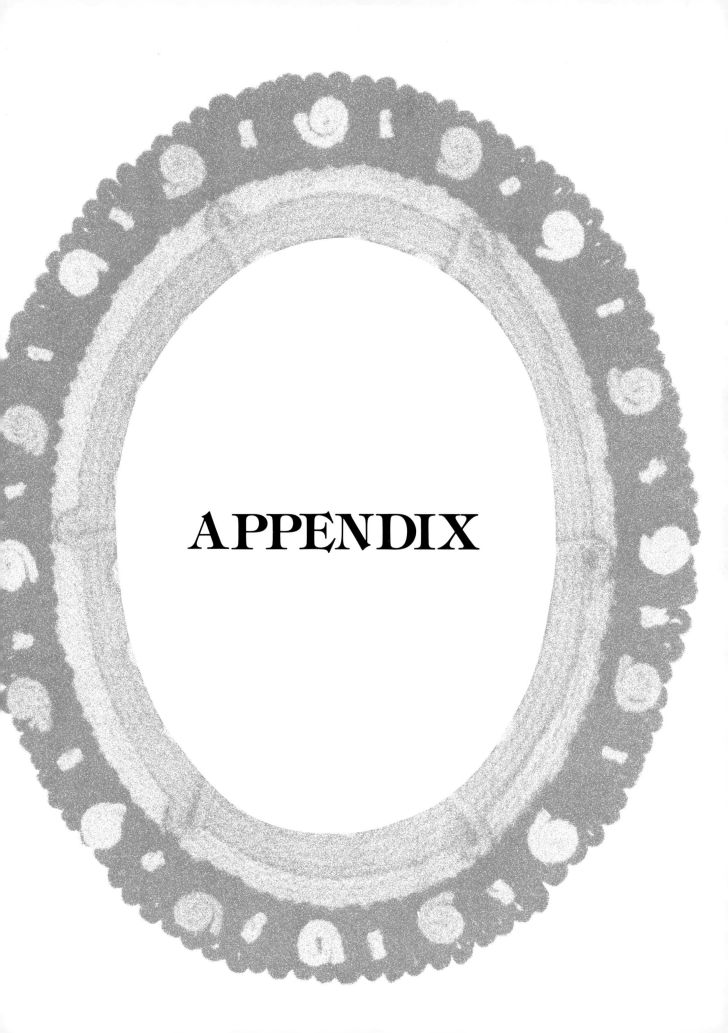

APPENDIX

Appendix — Professional Reference Guide

This reference guide is intended as a resource for obtaining information useful to professionals and their assistants, including occupational therapists, physical therapists, recreational therapists, those who are studying or working in the field of gerontology, arts and crafts instructors, and volunteers working with older adults in recreational arts and crafts programs.

PRIVATE ORGANIZATIONS

The listing includes private organizations that have responded to our questionnaire indicating that they sponsor recreational or educational programs, offer services, or issue publications for or pertaining to the elderly.

American Alliance for Health, Physical Education, and Recreation (AAHPER)
1201 16th Street, N.W.
Washington, D.C. 20036
A committee has been formed to study services for the aging.

American Association of Homes for the Aging
374 National Press Building
14th and F Streets, N.W.
Washington, D.C. 20045
Represents nationally the nonprofit homes and facilities for the aging; offers educational programs to enhance the professional expertise of its members in offering quality service to the aging.

American Association for Rehabilitation Therapy
P.O. Box 93
North Little Rock, Arkansas 72116
Advances the practice of rehabilitation, establishes and advances the standards of education and training of rehabilitation therapists, and encourages and promotes research.
Publications: *The Bulletin* — a publication for the general membership. *The Archives* — a professional journal featuring articles on all phases of rehabilitation.

American Association of Retired Persons/National Retired Teachers' Association
1909 K Street, N.W.
Washington, D.C. 20049
Reports worthy activities and projects of existing local clubs and groups for the aging and senior citizens organizations. Affords opportunities by qualified persons or agencies for the investigation and interchange of opinion and information of special interest in gerontology.
Publications: *Modern Maturity, Dynamic Maturity,* monthly news bulletin, bimonthly *NRTA Journal,* legislative information bulletin, leadership cassettes.

American Camping Association, Incorporated
Bradford Woods
Martinsville, Indiana 46151
"Member" camps offer camping programs for the aging.
Publications: *Camping Magazine* — contains periodic articles for those working with the aging. Listing of camps available upon request.

American Foundation for the Blind
15 West 16th Street
New York, New York 10011
Serves as a nonprofit clearing-house for information about blindness. Offers consultation, information and training materials, guidelines, research, and demonstration for the aging. Automatic needle-threaders and other products to aid the visually handicapped are sold. Write to the Foundation for a listing of publications.
Publication: *New Outlook for the Blind,* published monthly except for July and August.

American Health Care Association
Council of Activity Coordinators
1200 15th Street, N.W.
Washington, D.C. 20005
Responds to the needs and concerns of activity coordinators in long-term care facilities in order to promote a full and meaningful life for long-term care residents.

American Medical Association
Committee on Aging
535 North Dearborn Street
Chicago, Illinois 60610
Studies factors affecting the day-to-day lives of the elderly; collects and disseminates medical knowledge pertaining to health care for the aging; promotes the idea that there is no disease specifically attributable to the aging process; tries to eliminate segregation by reason of age in all fields of activity.

American Occupational Therapy Association
6000 Executive Building
Rockville, Maryland 20852
Promotes the professionalism of occupational therapy.
A list of publications and audio-visual materials is available upon request.

American Physical Therapy Association
1156 15th Street
Suite 500
Washington, D.C. 20055
Meets the physical therapy needs of people through development and improvement of physical therapy education, practice, and research.
A list of publications is available upon request.

The Arthritis Foundation
475 Riverside Drive
New York, New York 10027
Seeks the cause, prevention, and cure for arthritis through research programs, patient services, public health information and education, professional education, and training.
A list of publications and audio-visual materials is available on request.

Association of Medical Rehabilitation Directors and Coordinators, Incorporated
3830 Linklea Drive
Houston, Texas 77025
Unites psychiatrists and directors, coordinators and administrative officers of those clinics that treat the disabled; supervises rehabilitation and recreation and offers physical therapy, occupational therapy, etc., in clinic settings.
The association publishes a quarterly bulletin.

Gerontological Society
Suite 520, One DuPont Circle
Washington, D.C. 20036
The society is for professionals in the field of aging.
Publications: *Journal of Gerontology; The Gerontologist.*

Information and Research Utilization Center in Physical Education and Recreation for the Handicapped
c/o AAHPER, 1201 16th Street, N.W.
Washington, D.C. 20036
This is a demonstration project that collects, describes, and distributes information and resources for health educators, physical educators, and recreation specialists.

Institute of Lifetime Learning
1346 Connecticut Avenue, N.W.
Washington, D.C. 20036
This school of continuing education for older adults is the educational arm of the National Retired Teachers' Association and the American Association of Retired Persons. The Institute of Lifetime Learning stimulates interest in continuing education for older persons, offers consultation services, sponsors extension institutes of lifetime learning in cooperation with educational institutions.

International Federation on Aging
1909 K Street, N.W.
Washington, D.C. 20049
This organization serves primarily as an educational institution to promote the cross-cultural exchange of new program ideas among practitioners and organizations involved in servicing the aging, and serves as a regional and international advocate for the aging.

National Council of Senior Citizens, Incorporated
1627 K Street, N.W.
Washington, D.C. 20006
To win a better life for older Americans, the Council seeks social security benefits at a meaningful level, health security legislation for all Americans including the elderly, and modern housing within the means of the low-income elderly.
Publication: *Senior Citizen News* — a monthly newspaper.

National Geriatrics Society
212 West Wisconsin Avenue, Third Floor
Milwaukee, Wisconsin 53203
The society provides a means for professionals to keep in touch with developments in medicine, nursing rehabilitation, pharmacology, and psychology and the social sciences. The society is dedicated to the advancement of techniques of long-term care for the aged, infirm, chronically ill, handicapped, and convalescent patients.
Publications: *Geriatrics: Target 1980; Nursing Procedure Manual; Nursing Care/Requirements in Nursing Homes in the States of the Union; Views and News* — a monthly newsletter.

New York Association for the Blind (The Lighthouse)
111 East 59th Street
New York, New York 10022
A voluntary, nonprofit agency serving greater New York and offering direct service to all blind and visually impaired individuals. Their broad program encompasses a full education schedule, recreation programs, and summer camp.
A listing of publications is available upon request.

Therapeutic Recreation Information Center
University of Oregon
1607 Agate Street
Eugene, Oregon 97403
A computer-based information acquisition, storage and retrieval, and dissemination center specifically concerned with published and unpublished materials related to recreation services to ill, disadvantaged, disabled, and aging persons. Provides comprehensive annotated bibliographic reference materials to educators, researchers, students, practitioners, or others interested in therapeutic recreation for special groups in need of services.

VASCA — Vacation for the Aging and Senior Centers Association
225 Park Avenue South
New York, New York 10009
An agency for improving the quality of leisure-time services for the aging, with emphasis on senior centers and camps.

World Leisure and Recreation Association
345 East 46th Street
New York, New York 10017
This organization maintains a central service office for the world's recreation agencies; provides field service to countries desiring help with organizing national and regional agencies; and stresses importance of trained leadership for recreation so that the handicapped, ill, and aging everywhere can find life more rewarding.

PUBLIC AGENCIES

FEDERAL

Health, Education, and Welfare
330 Independence Avenue, S.W.
Washington, D.C. 20201

STATE

The following state offices on aging (listed alphabetically by state) help fund recreational programs for the aged. We recommend that you write to your state office on aging to receive your state publications and find out the local agency that may help you further.

Commission on Aging
402-C State Highway Building
Montgomery, Alabama 36104

Office of Aging
Division of Public Welfare
Department of Health and Welfare
Pouch H
Juneau, Alaska 99801

Division for Aging
State Department of Public Welfare
1624 West Adams Street
Phoenix, Arizona 85007

Office of Aging
State Capitol Building
Little Rock, Arkansas 72201

California Office on Aging
918 J Street
Sacramento, California 95814

Division of Services for the Aging
Department of Social Services
1600 Sherman Street
Denver, Colorado 80203

Department on Aging
90 Washington Street, Room 312
Hartford, Connecticut 06115

Special Assistant for Service to the Aged
Department of Public Welfare
122 C Street, N.W., Room 803
Washington, D.C. 20001

Division of Family Services
Department of Health and Rehabilitation Services
P.O. Box 2050
Jacksonville, Florida 32203

Division of Special Programs
Office of Aging, 618 Ponce De Leon Avenue
Atlanta, Georgia 30306

Office of Aging
Department of Public Health and Social Services
Government of Guam, P.O. Box 2816
Agana, Guam 96910

Commission on Aging
250 South King Street, Room 601
Honolulu, Hawaii 96813

Office on Aging
Capitol Annex #7
509 North 5th Street, Room 100
Boise, Idaho 83702

Department on Aging
2401 West Jefferson
Springfield, Illinois 62702

Commission on the Aging and Aged
1015 New State Office Building
Indianapolis, Indiana 46204
Newsletter: "Mature Living"

Commission on Aging
State Office Building
Des Moines, Iowa 50319

Division of Services for the Aging
Department of Social Services
State Office Building
Topeka, Kansas 66612

Commission on Aging
207 Holmes Street
Frankfort, Kentucky 40601

Commission on the Aging
P.O. Box 44282, Capitol Station
Baton Rouge, Louisiana 70804

Services for Aging
Department of Health and Welfare
State House
Augusta, Maine 04330

Commission on Aging
State Office Building
301 West Preston Street
Baltimore, Maryland 21201
Publication: "The Outlook"

Elder Affairs Department
18 Tremont Street
Boston, Massachusetts 02108

Commission on Aging
1101 South Washington Avenue
Lansing, Michigan 48913

Governor's Citizens Council on Aging
Suite 204, Metro Square Building
7th and Roberts Streets
St. Paul, Minnesota 55101

Mississippi Council on Aging
P.O. Box 4232
Jackson, Mississippi 39216

Office of Aging
Department of Community Affairs
501 Jefferson Building
Jefferson City, Missouri 65101

Commission on Aging
Penkay Eagles Manor
715 Fee Street
Helena, Montana 59601

Advisory Committee on Aging
State House Station 94784
Lincoln, Nebraska 68509

Aging Services Program
515 East Musser Street
Room 113
Carson City, Nevada 89701

Council on Aging
P.O. Box 786
3 South Street
Concord, New Hampshire 03301
Publication: Newsletter

Division on Aging
Department of Community Affairs
P.O. Box 2768
Trenton, New Jersey 08625

Commission on Aging
408 Galisteo Street
Santa Fe, New Mexico 87501
Publication: Newsletter

New York State Office for the Aging
855 Central Avenue
Albany, New York 12206

Governor's Coordinating Council on Aging
Administration Building
213 Hillsborough Street
Raleigh, North Carolina 27603

Staff Assistant on Aging
Public Welfare Board
State Capitol Building
Bismarck, North Dakota 58501

Ohio Commission on Aging
34 North High Street
Third Floor
Columbus, Ohio 43215

Special Unit on Aging
Department of Public Welfare
Box 25352
Capitol Station
Oklahoma City, Oklahoma 73125
Publication: "Senior Oklahomans"

Oregon State Program on Aging
313 Public Service Building
Salem, Oregon 97310
Publication: "The Pioneer," quarterly newsletter

Office of Family Services
Department of Public Welfare
Health and Welfare Building
Harrisburg, Pennsylvania 17120
Newsletter: "Aging in Pennsylvania"

Puerto Rico Gericulture Commission
Department of Health
P.O. Box 9342
Santurce, Puerto Rico 00908

Community Coordinator on Aging
Department of Community Affairs
289 Promenade Street
Providence, Rhode Island 02908

Interagency Council on Aging
2414 Bull Street
Columbia, South Carolina 29201

State Planning Agency
State Capitol Building
Pierre, South Dakota 57501
Publication: Bimonthly newsletter

Commission on Aging
510 Gay Street
Capitol Towers
Nashville, Tennessee 37219

Governor's Committee on Aging
Box 12125
Capitol Station
Austin, Texas 78711

Aging Division of Social Services
345 South 600th Street
Salt Lake City, Utah 84111

Human Services Agency
Office on Aging
81 River
Montpelier, Vermont 05602

Commission on the Aging
Charlotte Amalie
P.O. Box 539
St. Thomas, Virgin Islands 08801

Commission on the Aging
9th Street Office Building
9th and Grace Streets
Richmond, Virginia 23219
Publication: "Challenger," quarterly newsletter

State Council on Aging
Department of Public Assistance
P.O. Box 1162
Olympia, Washington 98501

West Virginia Commission on Aging
State Capitol
Charleston, West Virginia 25305
Publication: "Age in Action"

Division on Aging
Department of Health and Social Services
Room 690
1 West Wilson Street
Madison, Wisconsin 53702
Publication: "Aging in the News,"
quarterly newsletter

SCHOOLS

The schools listed below offer degree programs in the following fields: occupational therapy (occupational therapy assistant), physical therapy (physical therapy assistant), recreation (recreational therapy, recreational administration, recreational leadership, therapeutic recreation), gerontology (social gerontology, gerontological psychology, gerontology and leisure education), nursing home administration, and vocational crafts. Most of these listings were compiled from our research of the following sources:

1) *American Universities and Colleges,* 11th edition, W. Todd Furniss, editor, American Council on Education, Washington, D.C., 1973
2) *The College Blue Book — Degrees Offered by College and Subject,* 15th edition, Macmillan Information, New York, 1975
3) American Occupational Therapy Association
4) American Physical Therapy Association
5) Correspondence with the state offices of higher education.

We sent questionnaires to each school on this list requesting information about its current programs and asking for catalogues. We have used the information from the completed questionnaires and from the catalogues in compiling the information provided in this section. In the cases in which the information given on the questionnaire conflicted with the information given in the catalogue, we quote the catalogue and assume that the questionnaire was perhaps filled out hastily. In a few cases we did not receive answers to our request for a catalogue and/or the questionnaire was not returned. In these instances, we relied on the information provided by the sources listed above rather than omit the listing.

We do not list the hundreds of schools, junior colleges, colleges, and universities that offer craft courses. Most often these courses are credited toward a degree in fine arts. We recommend that you refer to *Craft Sources — The Ultimate Catalog for Craftspeople* by Paul Colin and Deborah Lippman published by M. Evans and Company, New York, 1975, for a comprehensive listing of schools throughout the United States that offer craft courses.

SCHOOLS LISTED AND DESCRIBED ALPHABETICALLY BY STATE

Code for Degrees:
C — Certificate   A — Associate   B — Bachelor   M — Master   D — Doctorate

School	Degree	Program
1. University of Alabama in Birmingham 1919 7th Avenue South Birmingham, Alabama 35233	B B	Occupational Therapy Physical Therapy
2. Northern Arizona University Flagstaff, Arizona 85721	B	Occupational Therapy
3. Arkansas Polytechnic College Russelville, Arkansas 72801	B B	Recreational Leadership Therapeutic Recreation
4. State College of Arkansas School of Health Sciences 12th and Marshall Streets Little Rock, Arkansas 72201	B	Physical Therapy
5. University of Arkansas at Little Rock 33rd Street and University Avenue Little Rock, Arkansas 72201	B	Physical Therapy
6. California State University Allied Health Professions Physical Therapy Department Fresno, California 93710	B	Physical Therapy
7. California State University Long Beach Campus 6101 East 7th Street Long Beach, California 90801	B B B, M	Occupational Therapy Physical Therapy Recreation

8. California State University North Ridge Campus 1811 Nordhoff Street Northridge, California 91324	B	Physical Therapy
9. De Anza College 21250 Stevenscreek Boulevard Cupertino, California 95014	A A	Physical Therapy Assistant Recreation
10. El Camino College 16007 South Crenshaw Boulevard Torrence, California 90506	A A	Physical Therapy Assistant Recreation
11. Foothill College 12345 El Monte Los Altos Hills, California 94022	A A	Physical Therapy Assistant Recreational Leadership
12. Fullerton Jr. College 321 East Chapman Avenue Fullerton, California 92634	A A A	Occupational Therapy Physical Therapy Recreational Leadership
13. Golden West College 15744 Golden West Street Huntington Beach, California 92647	A	Recreational Leadership
14. Loma Linda University School of Health Related Professions Loma Linda, California 92354	B B	Occupational Therapy Physical Therapy
15. Los Angeles City College 855 North Vermont Los Angeles, California 90029	A	Occupational Therapy
16. Monterey Peninsula Junior College 980 Fremont Monterey, California 93940	A A A	Occupational Therapy Physical Therapy Recreation Technician
17. San Diego City College 1425 Russ Boulevard San Diego, California 92101	A A	Physical Therapy Assistant Recreational Leadership
18. San Francisco State University 1600 Holloway Avenue San Francisco, California 94132	B, M	Recreation and Leisure Studies
19. San Jose State University San Jose, California 95114	B, M B, M	Occupational Therapy Recreation
20. Southwestern College 5400 Otay Lakes Road Chula Vista, California 92010	A A	Physical Therapy Recreational Leadership
21. Stanford University Division of Physical Therapy School of Medicine Palo Alto, California 94205	B, M	Physical Therapy
22. University of California Berkeley School of Social Welfare Berkeley, California 94720	B, M, D	Social Welfare — Specialization for students working with and for the aging
23. University of California The Medical Center San Francisco, California 94122	C, B	Physical Therapy

24. University of Southern California University Park Los Angeles, California 90007	B, M C B, M M	(Proposed) Gerontology For professionals already working in a specific area of the field Occupational Therapy Physical Therapy
25. Colorado State University Fort Collins, Colorado 80521	B, M	Occupational Therapy
26. University of Colorado Boulder, Colorado 80302	B, M	Physical Therapy
27. Quinnipiac Community College Mount Carmel Avenue Hamden, Connecticut 06518	B	Occupational Therapy
28. University of Connecticut Storrs, Connecticut 06268	B, M, D M	Physical Therapy Social Gerontology
29. Palm Beach Junior College Lake Worth, Florida 33460	A	Occupational Therapy
30. St. Petersburg Junior College 6605 Fifth Avenue North St. Petersburg, Florida 33710	A	Physical Therapy Assistant
31. University of Florida Box 212 J. Hillis Miller Health Center Gainesville, Florida 32601	B B	Occupational Therapy Physical Therapy
32. Emory University School of Medicine Division of Allied Health Services Graduate Program in Physical Therapy Atlanta, Georgia 30322	M	Physical Therapy
33. Gainesville Junior College P.O. Box 1358 Gainesville, Georgia 30501	A A	Occupational Therapy Physical Therapy
34. Georgia State University 33 Gilmer Street, S.E. Atlanta, Georgia 30303	B	Physical Therapy
35. Medical College of Georgia Department of Physical Therapy School of Allied Health Sciences Augusta, Georgia 30902	B	Physical Therapy
36. University of Georgia Athens, Georgia 30601	B	Fine Arts with a concentration in Crafts
37. Belleville Area College 2555 West Boulevard Belleville, Illinois 62221	A	Physical Therapy Assistant
38. Central YMCA Community College Physical Therapy Assistant Program 211 West Wacker Drive Chicago, Illinois 60606	A	Physical Therapy Assistant
39. Chicago Medical School University of Health Sciences 2020 West Ogden Avenue Chicago, Illinois 60612	B	Physical Therapy

40. Illinois Central College Physical Therapist Assistant Program P.O. Box 2400 East Peoria, Illinois 61614	A A	Physical Therapist Assistant Occupational Therapist Assistant
41. Morraine Valley Community College 10900 South 88th Avenue Palo Hills, Illinois 60465	C A	Occupational Therapy Assistant Recreational Leadership
42. Morton College Cicero, Illinois 60650	A	Physical Therapy Assistant
43. Northwestern University Evanston, Illinois 60201	C, B	Physical Therapy
44. Southern Illinois University Carbondale Campus Carbondale, Illinois 62901	A B B	Physical Therapy Assistant Occupational Therapy Education-Recreation Major
45. Thornton Community College South Holland, Illinois 60473	C	Occupational Therapy Assistant
46. University of Illinois at the Medical Center 1737 West Polk Chicago, Illinois 60680	B	Occupational Therapy
47. University of Illinois Urbana Champaign Campus Urbana, Illinois 61801	B B, M	Crafts Recreation
48. Indiana University Division of Allied Health Sciences School of Medicine 1100 West Michigan Street Indianapolis, Indiana 46202	B, M A B, M C	Occupational Therapy Occupational Therapy Technology Physical Therapy Nursing Home Administration
49. Ellsworth Community College 1100 College Avenue Iowa Falls, Iowa 50126	A	Occupational Therapy
50. Kirkwood Community College 6301 Bowling Street, S.W. Cedar Rapids, Iowa 52406	A	Occupational Therapy Assistant
51. The University of Iowa Iowa City, Iowa 52242	C, M, D B, M	Physical Therapy Recreation Education with a concentration in Recreational Leadership Therapeutic Recreation
52. University of Kansas Lawrence, Kansas 66044	B	Occupational Therapy
53. Eastern Kentucky University Richmond, Kentucky 40475	B A, B, M, A	Occupational Therapy Recreation Vocational Crafts
54. University of Kentucky South Limestone Street Lexington, Kentucky 40506	A B	Human Services (3 Gerontology courses) Physical Therapy
55. Louisiana State University Medical Center Department of Physical Therapy School of Allied Health Professions 1190 Florida Avenue New Orleans, Louisiana 70119	B	Physical Therapy

56. Northeast Louisiana University 780 University Avenue Monroe, Louisiana 71201	B	Physical Therapy
57. Baltimore Community College 2901 Liberty Heights Avenue Baltimore, Maryland 21215	C, A A C, A	Occupational Therapy Assistant Physical Therapy Recreational Leadership
58. University of Maryland at Baltimore 660 West Redwood Street Baltimore, Maryland 21201	B B, M, D	Physical Therapy Recreation
59. Boston University 755 Commonwealth Avenue Boston, Massachusetts 02215	B, M B, M	Occupational Therapy Physical Therapy
60. Northeastern University 360 Huntington Avenue Boston, Massachusetts 02115	B	Physical Therapy
61. Simmons College 300 The Fenway Boston, Massachusetts 02155	C, B	Physical Therapy
62. Springfield Technical Community College 1 Armory Square Springfield, Massachusetts 01101	A	Physical Therapy Assistant
63. Tufts University Medford, Massachusetts 02155	B, M	Occupational Therapy
64. Alpena Community College 666 Johnson Street Alpena, Michigan 49707	A	Occupational Therapy
65. Eastern Michigan University Ypsilanti, Michigan 48197	B	Occupational Therapy
66. Kellogg Community College 450 North Avenue Battle Creek, Michigan 49017	A	Physical Therapy Assistant
67. College of St. Catherine 2004 Randolph St. Paul, Minnesota 55116	B	Occupational Therapy
68. College of St. Thomas 2115 Summit Avenue St. Paul, Minnesota 55105	B	Occupational Therapy
69. Mankato State College School of Health, Physical Education, and Recreation Mankato, Minnesota 56001	B	Physical Therapy
70. St. Mary's Junior College Physical Therapy Assistant Program 2600 South 6th Street Minneapolis, Minnesota 55406	A	Physical Therapy Assistant
71. University of Minnesota Minneapolis, Minnesota 55455	B B, M, D B C B, M	Occupational Therapy Physical Therapy Recreational Leadership Recreation for Special Groups Therapeutic Recreation

72. Penn Valley Community College
Kansas City, Missouri 64105

A   Physical Therapy Assistant

73. St. Louis University
1401 South Grand Boulevard
St. Louis, Missouri 63119

B   Physical Therapy

74. University of Missouri — Columbia
Columbia, Missouri 65201

B   Occupational Therapy
B, M   Recreation

75. Washington University
St. Louis, Missouri 63130

M, D   Gerontological Psychology
B   Occupational Therapy
B   Physical Therapy

76. Kearny State College
Kearny, Nebraska 68847

B   Physical Therapy
B   Recreation

77. University of New Hampshire
Durham, New Hampshire 03824

B   Occupational Therapy

78. Essex County College
376 Osborne Terrace
Newark, New Jersey 07112

A   Physical Therapy Assistant

79. Albany Medical College
47 New Scotland Avenue
Albany, New York 12208

C, B   Physical Therapy

80. Columbia University
116th Street & Broadway
New York, New York 10027

B, M   Occupational Therapy
C, B   Physical Therapy

81. Columbia University Teachers College
Box 102
New York, New York 10027

M   Community Recreation Services
M   Education with Specializations in "Services to the Aging," Gerontology and Leisure Education
D   Recreation and Related Community Service
M   Therapeutic Recreation Services

82. Hunter College
695 Park Avenue
New York, New York 10021

B, M   Physical Therapy

83. Ithaca College
Ithaca, New York 14850

B   Physical Therapy

84. Long Island University
Zeckendorf Campus
Brooklyn, New York 11201

M   Physical Therapy

85. Maria College
Albany, New York 12208

A   Occupational Therapy
A   Physical Therapy

86. Nassau Community College
Stewart Avenue
Garden City, New York 11530

A   Physical Therapy Assistant

87. New York University
Washington Square
New York, New York 10003

B   Manual Arts Therapy
B, M, D   Occupational Therapy
M, D   Physical Therapy
B, M, D   Recreational Leadership
B, M, D   Therapeutic Recreation

88. Russell Sage College
45 Ferry Street
Troy, New York 12180

B   Physical Therapy

89. State University of New York at Buffalo 3435 Main Street Buffalo, New York 14214	B, M B	Occupational Therapy Physical Therapy
90. State University of New York Downstate Medical Center 450 Clarkson Avenue Brooklyn, New York 11203	B B	Occupational Therapy Physical Therapy
91. State University of New York at Stony Brook Health Sciences Center Stony Brook, New York 11790	B	Physical Therapy
92. State University of New York Upstate Medical Center 766 Irving Avenue Syracuse, New York 13210	B	Physical Therapy
93. Central Piedmont Community College 1141 Elizabeth Avenue Charlotte, North Carolina 28204	A	Physical Therapy Assistant
94. Duke University Durham, North Carolina 27706	C, M	Physical Therapy
95. East Carolina University School of Allied Health and Social Professions Greenville, North Carolina 27834	B	Physical Therapy
96. University of North Carolina at Chapel Hill Chapel Hill, North Carolina 27514	B, M B, M M	Physical Therapy Recreation Administration Therapeutic Recreation
97. North Dakota State School of Science Wahpeton, North Dakota 58075	A	Occupational Therapy
98. University of North Dakota University Station Grand Forks, North Dakota 58201	B B	Occupational Therapy Physical Therapy
99. Cuyahoga Community College 2123 East 9th Street Cleveland, Ohio 44115	A A	Occupational Therapy Assistant Physical Therapy Assistant
100. Ohio State University 190 North Oval Drive Columbus, Ohio 43210	B, M B	Occupational Therapy Physical Therapy
101. Tulsa Junior College 10th and Boston Streets Tulsa, Oklahoma 74119	A	Physical Therapy Assistant
102. University of Oklahoma Health Sciences Center 800 Northeast 13th Street Oklahoma City, Oklahoma 73190	B	Occupational Therapy
103. Mount Hood Community College Gresham, Oregon 97030	C A	Occupational Therapy Assistant Physical Therapy Assistant
104. Lehigh County Community College Schnecksville, Pennsylvania 18078	A A	Occupational Therapy Assistant Physical Therapy Assistant

105. Mount Aloysius Junior College Cresson, Pennsylvania 16630	A	Occupational Therapy Assistant
106. University of Pennsylvania School of Allied Health Philadelphia, Pennsylvania 19104	B, C B, C	Occupational Therapy Physical Therapy
107. University of Puerto Rico Medical Sciences Campus at San Juan San Juan, Puerto Rico	B B	Occupational Therapy Physical Therapy
108. Baylor University Fort Sam Houston, Texas 78234	C, M	Physical Therapy
109. St. Philip's College San Antonio, Texas 78203	C, A A	Occupational Therapy Assistant Physical Therapy Assistant
110. Texas Women's University Institute of Health Sciences Denton, Texas 76204	B, M, C B, M	Occupational Therapy Physical Therapy
111. University of Utah University Street and Second S. Salt Lake City, Utah 84112	B	Physical Therapy
112. Southern Seminary Junior College Buena Vista, Virginia 24416	A	Occupational Therapy
113. Virginia Commonwealth University Richmond, Virginia 23284	C, B, M A, B	Occupational Therapy Physical Therapy
114. Green River Community College 12401 Southeast 320th Street Auburn, Washington 98002	A A	Occupational Therapy Assistant Physical Therapy Assistant
115. University of Puget Sound 1500 North Warner Tacoma, Washington 98416	C, B, M	Occupational Therapy
116. University of Washington Seattle, Washington 98195	B,M B	Occupational Therapy Physical Therapy
117. West Virginia University Morgantown, West Virginia 26506	B	Physical Therapy
118. Madison Area Technical College 211 North Carroll Street Madison, Wisconsin 53703	C	Occupational Therapy
119. Marquette University 615 North 11th Street Milwaukee, Wisconsin 53223	B	Physical Therapy
120. Mount Mary College 2900 Menomenee Parkway Milwaukee, Wisconsin 53222	B	Occupational Therapy
121. University of Wisconsin Madison Campus Madison, Wisconsin 53706	B	Occupational Therapy
122. University of Wisconsin 3203 North Downer Avenue Milwaukee, Wisconsin 53201	C, B	Occupational Therapy
123. Wisconsin State University Eau Claire Campus Eau Claire, Wisconsin 53701	B	Occupational Therapy

178

SCHOOLS LISTED BY CAREER PREPARATION PROGRAM

The numbers listed below under program headings refer to the schools noted above. Each school in the alphabetical listing has a number in front of it. Please refer to this number code for the college name, address, and degree program.

Crafts
36
47

Gerontological Psychology
75

Gerontology
24

Gerontology and Leisure Education
81

Human Services
54

Manual Arts Therapy
87

Nursing Home Administration
48

Occupational Therapy and Occupational Therapy Assistant

1	33	59	87	109
2	40	63	89	110
7	41	64	90	112
12	44	65	97	113
14	45	67	99	114
15	46	68	100	115
16	48	71	102	116
19	49	74	103	118
24	50	75	104	120
25	52	77	105	121
27	53	80	106	122
31	57	85	107	123

Physical Therapy and Physical Therapy Assistant

1	28	56	81	100
4	30	57	82	101
5	31	58	83	103
6	32	59	84	104
7	33	60	85	106
8	34	61	86	107
9	35	62	87	108
10	37	66	88	109
11	38	69	89	110
12	39	70	90	111
14	40	71	91	113
16	42	72	92	114
17	43	73	93	116
20	44	75	94	117
21	48	76	95	119
23	51	78	96	
24	54	79	98	
26	55	80	99	

Recreation

7	19	47	58	76
9	44	53	74	81
10				

Recreation Administration
96

Recreation and Leisure Studies
18

Recreation for Special Groups
71

Recreation Technician
16

Recreational Leadership

3	13	20	51	71
11	17	41	57	87
12				

Social Gerontology
28

Social Welfare
22

Therapeutic Recreation

3	71	81	87	96
51				

Vocational Crafts
53

GERONTOLOGY CENTERS AND INSTITUTES

The following centers and institutes on aging are located at various universities throughout the country.

Center for Gerontological Studies
102 Anderson Hall
University of Florida
Gainesville, Florida 32611

Rocky Mountain Gerontology Center
301 Behavioral Science Building
University of Utah
Salt Lake City, Utah 84112

University of Wisconsin
Institute on Aging
425 Henry Mall, Room 209
Madison, Wisconsin 53706

University of Southern California
Leonard Davis School of Gerontology
University Park
Los Angeles, California 90007

North Texas State University
Center for Studies on Aging
Box 13438
NTSU Station
Denton, Texas 76203

Ball State University
Institute of Gerontology
Teachers College Annex
Muncie, Indiana 61801

Institute of Gerontology
University of Michigan
Ann Arbor, Michigan 48105

Duke University's Center for the Study of Aging
  and Human Development
Durham, North Carolina 27706

Center of Leisure Studies
University of Oregon
1587 Agate Street
Eugene, Oregon 97403

Portland State University
Institute on Aging
P.O. Box 751
Portland, Oregon 97207

BIBLIOGRAPHY

This bibliography includes books, pamphlets, booklets, and periodicals that will be helpful to people working with the elderly in recreational settings or for those seeking career advancement in these fields. Please note that entries are listed alphabetically by title.

EDUCATION

1. Corbin, H. Dan, and William J. Tait, *Education for Leisure,* Prentice-Hall, Inc., Englewood Cliffs, N.J., 1973. This book explains the importance of being educated in how to spend your leisure time. Crafts are considered as an activity carried over into later years.

2. *Educational Program Ideas — Recreation for the Elderly,* University of the State of New York, Bureau of Continuing Education, Curriculum Development, Albany, N.Y., 1968. This fifty-five-page booklet describes the philosophy of group programs. Arts and Crafts is regarded as an important part of the program.

3. *Occupational Outlook Handbook 1974–75,* U.S. Department of Labor, Bureau of Labor Statistics Bulletin #1785, Washington, D.C. This book supplies sources of information about future employment statistics, educational requirements, and descriptions of various occupational groups.

The following books are sources of information about colleges and universities in the United States and the programs, courses of study, and degrees they offer.

1. *American Universities and Colleges,* 11th edition, W. Todd Furniss, editor, American Council on Education, Washington, D.C., 1973.

2. *The College Blue Book — Degrees Offered by College and Subject,* 15th edition, Macmillan Information, New York, N.Y., 1975.

3. *The College Blue Book — U.S. Colleges: Narrative Descriptions,* 15th edition, Macmillan Information, New York, N.Y., 1975.

BIBLIOGRAPHIES

1. *Occupational Literature,* Forrester, Gertrude; H. W. Wilson Co., New York, N.Y., 1971. A book of annotated bibliographies of literature pertaining to various occupations among which are listings for occupational and physical therapists.

2. *Publications — Administration on Aging, 1974,* Administration on Aging, U.S. Department of Health, Education and Welfare, Washington, D.C., 1974. A bibliography of publications issued by AOA. Single copies of all the publications listed are available without charge as long as the supply lasts.

3. *NCOA Publications List 1975,* National Council on the Aging, Washington, D.C., 1975.
   This booklet is an annotated bibliography of books, pamphlets, periodicals, and films published and distributed by the National Council on the Aging.

4. *Words on Aging 1970* and *More Words on Aging 1971* (supplement), Administration on Aging, U.S. Department of Health, Education and Welfare, Washington, D.C.
   These booklets are annotated bibliographies of selected periodicals and books containing references on aging, the process of aging, the economic aspects of aging, health and medical care, and social and environmental services.

VOLUNTEERS

1. *A Guide for Chairmen of Volunteers,* Division of Services for the Aging, State Department of Social Welfare, Topeka, Kans., 1965.
   This thirty-five-page booklet gives details on recruiting, organizing, and training volunteers to perform a variety of services for older people. Included are the following sample forms: volunteer application forms, service record, and certification.

2. *Reaching the Homebound or Bedbound in One-to-One Contacts,* Department of Health and Social Services, Madison, Wis.
   This booklet describes motivational techniques in stimulating the homebound or bedridden.

3. *The Volunteer and the Older Person — A Handbook for Volunteers in the field of Aging,* Services for the Aging, Kansas State Department of Social and Rehabilitating Services, Topeka, Kans.
   This handbook describes ways in which volunteers can provide services to older people. Included are sections on leadership, how to relate to older people, and how to help older people.

SENIOR CENTERS, CLUBS, NURSING HOME RECREATION PROGRAMS

1. Merrill, Toni, M.A., *Activities for the Aged and Infirm: A Handbook for the Untrained Worker,* Charles C. Thomas, Springfield, Ill., 1972.
   This book includes over 200 activities that a volunteer can provide for senescent, bed-care, visually handicapped, wheelchair, and ambulatory patients.

2. *A Time to Enjoy — Recreation for Senior Citizens,* North Carolina Department of Natural and Economic Resources, Box 27687, Raleigh, N.C., 1974.
   This pamphlet states the qualifications both a professional and a volunteer should possess to run a successful recreation program for senior citizens. Arts and crafts play an important role in these recreation programs.

3. Vickery, Florence E., A.C.S.W., *Creative Programming for Older Adults — A Leadership Training Guide,* Association Press, New York, N.Y., 1972.
   This book explains the qualities of a leader and includes a chapter on creative activities for senior citizens. The activities include arts and crafts, drama, music, and creative writing.

4. *Guide for Year Round Program Planning for Senior Citizens Groups,* Commission on Aging, State of Iowa, State Office Building, Des Moines, Iowa.
   This booklet describes the purpose and the planning of a senior citizens organization.

5. *Information on How to Organize a Senior Citizens Club and Facts on the Older Population in Rhode Island,* Division on Aging, 150 Washington Street, Providence, R.I., 1966.
   This pamphlet describes the objectives of a senior citizens club, leadership qualifications, hints for leaders, and suitable meeting places.

6. *NCOA Publications List 1975,* National Council on the Aging, Washington, D.C., 1975.
   This booklet is an annotated bibliography of NCOA's literature on the following topics: aging, community programs, planning, services, employment and retirement, housing and living arrangements, multipurpose and senior centers, protective services, brochures, and periodicals. The organization publishes a large amount of worthwhile material. Since we cannot include listings of all the published material here, we did not list any other NCOA publication individually. *NCOA Publications List 1975* is a forerunner to a more comprehensive list to be published in the near future.

7. Merrill, Toni, *Old Timers' Club,* Wisconsin Division of Family Services, 1 West Wilson St., Madison, Wis., 1975.
   This booklet describes specific program activities for twenty-four sessions of a senior club.

8. Stein, Thomas A., and Douglas Sessoms, *Recreation and Special Populations,* Holbrook Press, Inc., Boston, Mass., 1973.
   Sections of this book pertain to recreational craft programs for the aged and handicapped.

9. Williams, Arthur, *Recreation for the Aging,* Association Press, New York, N.Y., 1962. Prepared for the National Recreation Association. This book explains the senior citizen's need for recreation as a way of feeling needed. Hobbies and crafts are considered an important part of the recreation program because they provide a personal satisfaction that is matched by few other activities. The general physical disabilities of aging are mentioned but they are not considered hindrances to recreational activities.

10. Pomeroy, Janet, *Recreation for the Physically Handicapped*, The Macmillan Co., New York, N.Y., 1964.
Sections of this book pertain to handicaps common to the aged and craft activities suitable for people with such handicaps. For example, pottery, sand painting, and mosaics are described in detail.

11. Lucas, Carol, *Recreation in Gerontology,* Charles C. Thomas, Springfield, Ill., 1964.
This book is also a guide for establishing or expanding programs of activity for older people.

12. Williams, Arthur, *Recreation in the Senior Years,* Association Press, New York, N.Y., 1962.
This book restates the same ideas as Mr. Williams' other book, *Recreation for the Aging.*

13. Lucas, Carol, *Recreational Activity Development for the Aging in Homes, Hospitals and Nursing Homes,* Charles C. Thomas, Springfield, Ill., 1962.
This book is a guide to establishing effective programs and provides stimuli for existing programs.

14. O'Neill, Virginia, *Senior Centers — Definition and Description of Senior Centers,* American Public Welfare Association, 1313 East 60th St., Chicago, Ill.
This seventeen-page booklet is divided into two categories: a guide for organizing and operating a senior center and senior centers in an urban setting.

15. Merrill, Toni, M.A., *365 Things to Talk About in a Nursing Home*, Charles C. Thomas, Springfield, Ill., 1974.

CRAFTS

1. Fish, Harriet U., *Activities Programs for Senior Citizens,* Parker Publishing Company, Inc., West Nyack, N.Y., 1971.
This book describes how to work with senior citizens in arts and crafts programs as well as other recreational programs. The author describes suitable types of projects for older men and women, types of craft products to use, and how to compensate for some physical disabilities of older adults.

2. Lyon, Mary, *Crafts for Retirement: A Guidebook for Teachers and Students,* American Craftsmen's Council, 1962, 1964. (A reprint is anticipated.)
This book describes various craft areas suitable for the retired.

3. Gould, Elaine and Loren, *Crafts for the Elderly,* Charles C. Thomas, Springfield, Ill., 1971.
This book presents a series of handcraft projects that can be used in nursing homes, senior centers, or at home.

4. Colin, Paul, and Deborah Lippman, *Craft Sources — The Ultimate Catalog for Craftspeople,* M. Evans & Co., Inc., New York, N.Y., 1975.
A detailed craft guide that includes an annotated bibliography of available books, magazines, organizations, and supplies, categorized according to over thirty craft fields. The book is illustrated with photos and graphics. Excerpts from craft books and interviews with craft people give depth and clarity to the craft field descriptions. Descriptive listings of schools offering craft courses are listed by state.

5. Ickis, Marguerite, *Handicrafts and Hobbies for Recreation and Retirement,* Dodd, Mead and Company, New York, N.Y., 1960.
This book describes woodworking, leathercraft, ceramics, copper enameling, lapidary work, mosaics, tapestry weaving, sandcraft, rugmaking, etc.

6. Rich, M.K., *Handicrafts for the Homebound Handicapped,* Charles C. Thomas, Springfield, Ill., 1970.
This book describes handicrafts that can be adapted to meet the needs of the handicapped.

7. Glassman, Judith, *The National Guide to Craft Supplies,* Van Nostrand Reinhold Company, New York, N.Y., 1975.
This book is a complete mail-order shopping guide of over 600 sources classified into forty-two craft areas (macrame, woodworking, lapidary work, etc.). There is an annotated directory of 600 entries of craft bookstores, societies, organizations, galleries and museums, places of instruction, craft fairs, and periodicals. In addition, there is a bibliography of over 800 craft books, but none has been annotated.

PROFESSIONAL PERIODICALS

1. *Aging,* U.S. Department of Health, Education and Welfare, Office of Human Development, Administration on Aging. Published monthly; $5.50 per year. Editor: James E. Warner.

2. *Current Literature on Aging,* published by NCOA quarterly; free to NCOA members; $3.00 per year to others or 75¢ per copy.

3. *Memo,* published monthly by NCOA National Institute of Senior Centers; free on request; includes program ideas, news of specific center programs, legislation information, and listings of helpful publications.

4. *Therapeutic Recreation Journal,* Lawhead Press, Inc., Athens, Ohio. Published quarterly.

CRAFT PERIODICALS

1. *Aunt Jane's,* Tower Press, Inc., Box 428, Seabrook, N.H. Published quarterly; $2.00 per year. Editor: Evelyn Schoolcraft.
Magazine has sewing and craft ideas.

2. *Creative Crafts,* P.O. Box 700, Newton, N.J. Published bimonthly; $4.50 for six issues; single copies are 75¢ at newsstands. Editor: Sybil C. Hays.
General crafts are included.

3. *Decorating and Craft Ideas Made Easy,* 1001 Foch Street, Fort Worth, Tex. Published ten times a year; $8.00 for one year; $15.00 for two years; $21.00 for three years.
Includes general crafts.

4. *Hobbies and Things Magazines,* 30915 Loraine Road, North Olmstead, Ohio. Published bimonthly; $4.00 per year. Editor: Karen Joseph.
Includes general crafts.

5. *McCall's Needlework and Crafts,* The McCall Pattern Co., 230 Park Avenue, New York, N.Y. Published biannually; $1.50 per issue. Mostly needlecrafts with some popular craft ideas.

6. *Popular Needlework,* Tower Press, Inc., Box 428, Seabrook, N.H. Editor: P. J. Farbuck. Includes various needlework crafts.

7. *Woman's Day — 101 Craft Ideas,* Fawcett Publications, Inc., Fawcett Building, Greenwich, Conn.; 95¢ per copy. Editor: Dan Blue. Includes needlework and crafts.

8. *Woman's World, Money-savers,* Family Crafts. Published monthly by Woman's World Joint Venture; $9.00 per year. Editor: Holly Garrison.
Includes scrap craft ideas.

9. *Woman's World, Money-savers,* Needle Arts. Published monthly by Woman's World Joint Venture; $9.00 per year. Editor: Holly Garrison.
Includes all types of needlework.